AF538245

A. Lynn Scoresby

Deseret Book Company
Salt Lake City, Utah

Printed in the United States of America

First printing April 1986

Library of Congress Cataloging-in-Publication Data

Scoresby, A. Lynn.
Foundations for a happier marriage.

Includes index.
1. Marriage. 2. Communication in marriage.
I. Title.
HQ734.S4428 1986 646.7'8 86-2082
ISBN 0-87579-023-2

CONTENTS

1

SHARING IN MARRIAGE

As I entered the hospital and walked down the corridor to the adolescent psychiatric unit, I thought about the young person I had come to see. She was not yet fourteen years old, but she had been sent to the hospital by the juvenile authorities. Officially, she was in trouble because her abuse of alcohol and drugs had brought her to a crisis: she had consumed so much alcohol that she had passed out during school. Without proper medical care, she could have died from what she had done. Yet this behavior was really only the result of a far deeper pain.

I knew that since her parents' divorce three years before, this child had suffered continuously from the arguments going on between her mother and her father. The reasons for their divorce didn't matter to her. What mattered was that they had divorced and that they were still angry with one another—so angry, in fact, that they were quite unaware of how they affected this girl, her sisters, and her brothers. These parents either had forgotten or had never known that children have emotional ties to both parents. When parents separate or engage in considerable conflict, they cause painful, emotional division in the children that prevents them from living happy, normal lives.

I wondered if I could help create conditions that would allow this child to know the simple satisfactions of a stable life—going to school, doing homework, being with friends, and having a reasonable amount of contact with both her father and her mother. I knew it would be difficult. I have seen so many children in this situation, and I never fail to be saddened by it.

I know that for some couples divorce is better than remaining together. In rare instances, a divorce can even be better for the children than living with certain kinds of conflict. Far more often, however, divorce brings enormous pain to parents and children, creating a condition of instability that is difficult to repair. Children who must live with such instability may be unable to focus their energies constructively. They may begin to fail in school as their ability to concentrate and their desire for achievement lessen. They may become calloused and selfish because they have learned to manipulate parents by pitting one against the other to obtain privileges and possessions. I have known children who, because of parental conflict, have attempted suicide, and I have known a few who succeeded. For "the sake of the children" is no empty phrase—any couple in conflict should do all in their power to prevent the breakup of their family.

The children are not the only ones who suffer, though. I have seen mothers unprepared for wage earning, unable to find employment, humiliated when they have to seek welfare services from their church and state because the fathers no longer provide. I have seen other women in distress because their work outside the home has cost their children the companionship of the only parents left to them. Deprived of the emotional support required to live happily, families in such circumstances live a barren routine of sadness. When the situation could have been avoided, the tragedy is indeed great.

Beyond all of this, I know that people who experience divorce face a profound loneliness that takes many forms. As the word *divorce* implies, divorced people find themselves separate, alone. Even though there may be children or friends to occupy part of their time, there are no other intimately concerned adults with whom to share companionship. Many lonely hours can be spent in depressed silence. Loneliness can also stem from the shocking realization that there aren't many others who could be desirable companions. And, in spite of how exciting dating relationships may have seemed in memory, they seem surprisingly shallow and difficult for most people who have known the emotional depth of marriage. I have listened to women talk of their disgust and frustration when they are viewed as pieces of goods to be auctioned off at one or another singles' activity to the available men. I have heard lonely men, too, complain of the insincerity of many women.

As good as any other relationship may be, no other relationship has the potential for happiness and fulfillment that a good marriage has. Furthermore, any marriage can increase in happiness if productive effort is applied by husband or wife separately or, preferably, together.

I have ached for those I've known who have gone through the pain of divorce. I have wished I could give them something more than advice and solace. I have wished I could help them find ways to be happy together, to somehow give them the skills to change their lives. As I have searched the professional literature describing marriage as a place of love and happiness, I find virtually no educational programs available to help people prepare for such a state, nothing to help people learn what I have found in my personal life and in my counseling of others. That is, I find only inadequate descriptions of the need for and the process involved in preparing for cooperative, involved sharing. Marriage, above all else, requires us to share skillfully and in many ways in order for us to be happy.

WHAT IS MARRIAGE?

The first step in increasing marital happiness is understanding what marriage is. There are surprisingly many notions available to us about the nature of marriage. Some of these seem to me better than others in providing foundations for a happier marriage. In my experience, learning what marriage is and acting according to that knowledge enable couples to increase the satisfaction in their relationship.

In some ways, every marriage is different from any other because two people together create a unique personality for their marriage. But in other ways, all marriages are alike. I believe it is best to see marriage as a set of shared situations, created simply by the state of being married. Such situations provide some of life's most personal and profound experiences.

In using this definition, I assume that the married couple plan to live together under the same roof, in which case they will naturally share shelter, food, and worldly goods. But by "shared situations" I mean much more than these. Being married means we present many of our thoughts and feelings and most of our actions to each other. We share happily if we present them accurately and freely; we share unhappily if we withhold. In any case, we *do* share. In marriage, even silence and absence are shared, and even those who find ways to avoid involvement are sharing. (It is exceptionally ironic to me that people will marry to find companionship yet be unable or unwilling to acknowledge that they share a relationship and a responsibility for the quality of that relationship.) Sharing in marriage is not only unavoidable, but also determines the quality of our marriages.

As children or single adults, we are seldom required to share as much as happy marriages require us to share. Nor are we confronted very often with the need to learn that sharing also includes being separate, allowing another person time alone. The gradual process of learning to balance these two concepts—creating intimacy and allowing separateness—is the major task in building happy marriages.

Accepting the fact that we cannot *not* share in marriage, our only choice, if we want happiness, is to learn more fully and more accurately how to disclose our own thoughts and feelings and how to understand what is disclosed to us. One difficulty with this is that the major sharing situations in marriage involve life's most personal and profound experiences. However difficult though, sharing in marriage results in some of life's greatest rewards. I have summarized six of the most common areas of sharing in marriage (see Table 1):

1. The sexual relationship is vitally important in marriage. The kind of sharing involved in the sexual relationship covers much more than the mechanical acts of intercourse. A sexual relationship between husband and wife is all of the affection,

warmth, and sexual communication that they experience. To some degree every husband and wife experience the need to share sexually with each other and will pattern their sexual relationship in ways to suit themselves.

2. The obligations, privileges, and decisions related to the management of money and resources comprise another area of mandatory sharing. Again, the way a married couple share may be based on their own preferences or past experiences, but every couple will choose some system of money management and will share in the discussion of problems they have about money.

3. Married couples also share in decisions and requirements relating to child care. Even those who have no children, by choice or misfortune, will be involved in sharing the experience of childlessness. Child care is one situation that is so complex for many couples it alone consumes much of their time and energy.

4. Married people must also share in social experiences with one another, together with others, and separately with others. Their social experiences include friendships, vacations and other recreation, and all types of social events and obligations.

5. A couple must also come to some kind of agreement concerning religious matters, whether one or both spouses will be involved in an established pattern of religious worship through a church, or whether one or both will have little or no identifiable religious beliefs. Since religious beliefs generally have some bearing on the behavior and moral instruction of children, the area is a difficult one to ignore.

6. Marriage requires that each person begin a relationship with the spouse's relatives. The quality of the marriage influences and is affected by the way a couple share time and resources with their extended families.

SKILLS IN SHARING

Like many boys, I learned early to believe that talking about or showing my feelings was not manly. Through athletic competition or through arguments with other boys, I had felt ridiculed for showing any fear, hurt, or sadness. As a result, I

Table 1
Six Primary Areas Shared in Marriage

Areas	What We Share
1. Sexual relationship	All forms of (or lack of) affection, warmth, expressions of love, sexual activity
2. Money and resources	All activities, conversations, and management skills related to money, possessions, and resources needed for living
3. Child care	All activities, discipline, teaching times, conversation involved with the rearing of children (also the inadequacies, uninvolvement, and indifferences between parent and child)
4. Social activities	All social events, together or as individuals, all friendships, and all relationships with business and personal acquaintances
5. Religious activities	All religious beliefs and all participation or nonparticipation in religious activities
6. Relatives	Time spent with and thoughts and feelings concerning parents (natural parents and in-laws), grandparents, and other close relatives

learned to avoid open displays of my emotions by isolating myself from other people.

Later, after I had been married for a while, I found myself facing the pressures of graduate school, work, and church callings, and experiencing more stress than I had ever experienced before. The pressure resulted in depression, frustration, and anxiety. Rather than try to express these feelings or allow them to come out inappropriately, I often came home for the evening and withdrew, sometimes sitting in front of the television set and other times retiring to my private study room. After I had done this many times, my wife told me that she was unhappy because she felt I did not need her. This astounded me because I felt her care of me and our children was vital to my success in graduate school. I knew how much I needed her in other ways too. I couldn't understand how she would not know this.

I realized, however, that because I would not share with her, in this case talk about my feelings, she did not know how to participate with me. She wisely made a direct request, asking me to talk to her more often. To my surprise, I found this very difficult, especially talking about things that seemed quite personal, but I made several attempts and was finally able to share what I was thinking and feeling. I discovered that having someone listen not only helped me, but also allowed my wife to participate comfortably in what was happening to me. Since then I have been able to refine my abilities, and now I enjoy talking with my wife about many things I had never imagined I could share. In other words, I know from experience that skills in sharing can be learned, and learning them reaps a rich reward.

In attempting to evaluate the needs of a happy marriage, I have found that skill in the following eight areas is extremely beneficial: talking and listening, showing commitment, receiving love, making love last, discovering new rewards, using differences, reducing anger, and accepting with hope.

Talking and Listening

One foundation for marital happiness is an ability to understand combined with a confidence of being understood. This reciprocation allows a couple to continuously incorporate the discoveries they make about each other into the actual way they live. Through understanding and being understood a couple may find peace of mind, and by engaging in the talking and listening that permit understanding to occur, any married person can improve the quality of his or her marriage.

Showing Commitment

Healthy human beings are active: they *do* things. What they do reveals the nature of their commitments; and how they use their time shows where their interests are. Husbands and wives can often measure the satisfaction they find in their marriages by the acts of commitment they show to the marriage relationship. For instance, comparing the amount of time devoted to the marriage with the amount of time spent on other things will help determine the level of commitment. If the commitment to the marriage is weak, if a companion is ignored in order to do other things, the relationship will quickly become less satisfying.

One young married couple described the following situation. The wife was very unhappy. Before they were married, the husband had spent a great deal of time for many years with a small group of close friends. These young men assumed that their companionship would continue after marriage as it had existed before marriage. As an example of her frustrations, the wife told of a time when she and her husband were watching television and had begun to be affectionate. Just at the moment when they had decided to extend their affection to something more intimate, they heard a car horn. Her husband said, "Oh, that's the guys," and, putting on a coat, he opened the door and left. He was, of course, a bit embarrassed, but he was still confused as to why she was frustrated. He failed to see the situation as an act of uncommitment.

There are numerous acts of commitment that can be expressed throughout marriage. Learning how to express them and choosing to do so increase sharing and happiness.

Receiving Love

It is quite common for children to worry about whether they are or can be loved by another person. Many individuals who are unhappy in marriage have had experiences that reinforced that childhood worry: they have grown up fearing they cannot be loved. When people are unable to believe in their own lovableness, two things generally happen. The first is that fearful people tend to respond to the unloving behavior of their partners more readily than to expressions of love. The second is that the inadequate reception of love stifles further expressions of love in the relationship. If a husband, for example, tries to communicate that he loves his wife, but his wife cannot receive the message, he will eventually discontinue his expressions for lack of response. Then, if she expresses love less often because he is seldom expressing love, their relationship will become even more barren.

Both spouses should examine themselves to determine whether they fear they are unlovable. Admitting such a fear can lead to a resolution of it. Failure to resolve the fear can lead to blaming problems on the partner and arguing over who is at fault. Gaining confidence that we are loved and learning to accept love from another person are major steps in making marriage more satisfying.

Making Love Last

A marriage may be the only situation we enter into with the understanding or hope that we will be loved and be required to love. Love and marriage are inextricably interwoven. Couples who express love frequently report more satisfaction than those couples who express it infrequently. Nearly everyone accepts this idea; yet many still fail to express love to their partners or to improve how they do it.

Ensuring that those I love know I love them is vitally important to me. It gives me a great deal of peace and satisfaction when I know that my wife truly understands how much I love her. This requires that I express my love for her in many different and new ways. Any couple can improve the quality of their marriage by making sure that both know love is still there and still strong.

Discovering New Rewards

Our involvement with one another increases according to the amount of security and safety we feel with each other. As our lives continue together, this increased involvement is fertile ground for a continuous discovery of what makes us happy. Many people focus so much attention on their problems and conflicts that they fail to think about, let alone emphasize, what they find of value. Even though we all give lip service to the idea that marriages should be happy, many of us refuse to look for the positive aspects of marriage and to experiment in order to increase the number of things we find rewarding.

One husband reported, that for many years, his wife had invited him to go for walks in the evening. Since he saw no practical purpose in doing this, he always refused, saying that he had other important things to do. One day, with nothing to do, he relented. He walked with his wife down their street and out into a wooded area near their home. As they walked they began to talk, and their conversation continued through the paths in the nearby park. Because she had taken this route on other occasions, she could point out to him several little places of beauty. He felt himself relax and began to appreciate the companionship and his wife's view of nature. It took them approximately thirty-five minutes. Arriving home, they both felt closer, and he felt relieved of much of the pressure he had brought home from his day's work. He said, "I never thought I would stop doing some business in order to go for a walk with my wife, but I found it to be one of the most rewarding things we have ever done together. I look forward to those walks and have even taken a day or two off each year just so we could walk alone in the park and in the nearby mountains."

This man's experience shows how easy it is to discover new rewards. Though we may not find walking together as rewarding as this couple did, we can uncover areas that appeal especially to us. Unfortunately, such areas in marriage will remain unknown if we fail to look for them. Discovering new rewards is a fairly simple thing to do, and increasing the number of rewarding events we share will improve the quality of our married life.

Using Differences

We often think that we argue because we are different from each other, and so conclude that our differences cause us problems. We may fail to understand that our differences and their resolution spark our growth. To be happy we must learn to use our differences to strengthen our marriage.

This is not as difficult as we often think. We have only to learn patience and skill in making adjustments. The results will be two-fold: we will no longer argue about differences, and we will be more confident in our abilities to face what may yet come.

Differences do not mean disloyalty. They simply suggest an opportunity for us to grow.

Reducing Anger

Most anger is not useful, but many people believe it is all right to express it. In fact, many married people do better at learning new ways to express their anger than they do learning new ways to express love. Learning ways to reduce the amount of time we spend feeling angry can increase our ability to share.

Fear of becoming angry is also a common reason for not sharing. It seems better to many to avoid talking or participating with their spouses, at least temporarily, so that anger will not erupt. Couples may end up not sharing in money management or in rearing their children, for example, simply to avoid anger. Unfortunately, this strategy diminishes happiness. More importantly, avoidance of anger perpetuates the problem. Any problem that could be resolved at one stage simply takes on added dimensions when it is left unsolved to continue to plague the marriage.

Viewing anger reduction as an important sharing skill, we can work to associate with one another without "blowing up" or "getting out of sorts." Much of anger reduction can be a matter of conscious control, just deciding not to get angry, to talk calmly instead. Frequently, however, we must understand what causes anger in order to decrease it. Then, when we learn ways to resolve those causes, we will have increased our ability to share the marriage in happiness.

Accepting with Hope

I have often wondered why some couples fail to realize that the anger and intense frustration they feel would not exist if there were not a great deal of love between husband and wife. We do not usually get angry at people for whom we feel indifference. More often we become angry at the ones we care about, or from whom we expect things, and with whom we fail. It is no surprise that marriage partners produce such intensity of feeling in each other. We could realize that the very anger we feel toward our partners is an indication of the amount of hope we should have for the continuation of the marriage relationship. The challenge is learning how to turn this hurt into happiness.

One way of doing this is to learn how to express acceptance and hope. Most of the time, this means to simply stop trying to make something of our partners that they are not and to recognize the value of what is there. In other words, we learn to acknowledge exactly what we are and what our companions are and to remove from our thoughts and conversation the notion that they should be or should not be something else. Acceptance of what is, combined with hope for improvement in the relationship, precedes any change. It is an important sharing skill.

If we add this skill to those for reducing anger, using differences, discovering new rewards, making love last, receiving love, showing commitment, and talking and listening, we can increase the emotional value of the shared marital experience. This will allow a marriage to grow into a relationship that provides two people with life's greatest satisfactions. Throughout the rest of the book, I will describe these sharing skills and apply them to the six general areas of sharing: sexual relationship, money and resources, child care, social activities, religious activities, and relatives.

2

TALKING AND LISTENING

Books about marriage seldom fail to include a section about communication. This is because communication is so basic and such an important part of interpersonal satisfaction. The amount of information that couples are able to transmit between themselves is related to how happy and satisfied they are with their relationship.

Too often we form ideas about marriage that are based on preconceived images we have of typical personality traits: a dominant husband and submissive wife, or a controlling wife with hen-pecked husband, for instance. These images distract us from the more important tasks of seeing each person on his or her own merits and fostering good communication.

In childhood, a person begins to learn a talking style. Over a long period of time, this style develops to include the amount of talking a person feels comfortable about doing, the topics a person is informed about, and the situations in which a person will or will not talk. By adulthood, this style is quite stable and tends to resist much change.

A graduate student I supervised based his dissertation research on this idea. He found several married couples who were willing to participate in his study and gave them a test that measured the satisfaction they found in their family. He then sent each couple a set of cards with personal and interpersonal discussion topics written on them. The couples agreed to discuss one topic a day. At the conclusion of his study six weeks later, the student retested the participants to see if their satisfaction had increased or decreased. Those—both husbands and wives—who had discussed more of the topics reported the greatest increase in satisfaction.

Fortunately, marriage communication does not depend solely on talking. Satisfying communication is created not only when two people can disclose personal information, such as a husband's telling of his thoughts and feelings, but also when they can pay attention to events that occur between them.

Listening is also a learned trait. A listening style can be changed more easily than a talking style, however. Listening depends on one's willingness to patiently gather information while encouraging the speaker to continue talking. One could rightly expect that as listening skills improve, talking tends to become more accurate.

FAILURE TO COMMUNICATE ACCURATELY

The actual amount of talking and listening varies from marriage to marriage, but each couple, to be happy, has to find a suitable amount for them. Otherwise, one or both spouses experience increased confusion. When a couple spend little time in talking or listening, they feel greater anxiety because the likelihood for misinterpretation and doubt increases. For instance, a woman whose husband doesn't talk to her very often may wonder if he likes her. Consequently, when couples fail to share enough ideas and thoughts with each other or fail to share accurately, they increase the possibility that their anxiety will distort what they perceive about their marriages.

Such conclusions stem from the notion that a desire to talk is a form of expressing attraction. Conversely, failing to talk or to listen to someone who wants to talk is viewed as rejection or lack of consideration. Many couples have been able to improve their marriages by simply having two or three "marriage conferences" a week. These conferences are designed to last for thirty minutes, during which time each person is to ask the other a total of five questions, listening to the answers without interruption. Oftentimes a couple should establish the rule that the person who asks the questions cannot agree or disagree with any responses he hears—the listener can only state whether a message is understood. It is surprising how much good two or three half-hour marriage conferences will do for a couple who have previously avoided talking with each other.

Anyone who has been married will recognize that when feelings have been hurt, a common reaction is to refuse to discuss the situation. This refusal begins a self-enclosed cycle that can last a whole lifetime. Any frequently disputed subject can become associated with volatile emotions, and the same emotions will tend to reappear whenever the subject comes up again. A couple may then decide to not discuss the topic so as to avoid arguments, even though the failure to communicate well is what caused their unhappiness in the first place. Eventually, one person's thoughts and feelings are so distorted by inaccurate sending and poor listening that a sender cannot get an accurate message to the receiver. A couple in this situation have created a lasting problem.

When we are emotionally aroused, we usually distort what we say, and we do not understand clearly. We may speak forcibly or lose our sense of tact and consideration. We may become defensive, concentrating on warding off words rather than receiving them. We may verbally attack the other. Then, because we cannot solve the problem we argue about, we adopt a compensating strategy of separating ourselves, which suspends the fight but does not bring complete peace of mind. It is unfortunate that we allow these conditions to be created at all. Such a situation, however, is usually not unsolvable, and a couple who are willing to learn and rehearse certain skills can change their relationship into one of accurate talking and clear understanding.

WHAT TO TALK ABOUT

All of the shared situations in marriage involve expectations about how people should act. These expectations are formed from observations, ideas, and other information accumulated as we grow from childhood to maturity. Here is a simple example: If a husband's parents had a clear separation between "men's work" and "women's work," the husband might enter marriage expecting the relationship to conform to his experience. His justification for not involving himself in some domestic duties would be that they were not his work, but his wife's. This example, although simple, is still part of many marriages, even in this day of "raised consciousness," even when wives work outside the home. Many working women, knowing they work the same hours and carry the same load as their husbands, expect their husbands to share more domestic responsibility. Yet there is evidence that wives who work outside the home are still left, because of long-standing cultural expectations, with a preponderance of the domestic duties.

There are many other common marital expectations. In regard to a sexual relationship, most people in North American society come into marriage expecting that sex is something a male does *to* and *for* his wife and that the wife should make herself available. Women generally expect men to find them attractive and sexually desirable; men are often expected to initiate encounters.

I am not suggesting that these expectations are morally or psychologically correct. I am only proposing that these are commonly held expectations. In any case, one of the most important things to be talked about in any shared situation is what the husband expects of his wife and what the wife expects of her husband.

When a husband and wife can tell what they want from each other, they can see more clearly and begin to make the necessary adjustments in their behavior or their expectations. I know of a woman who complained that her husband was a crude and clumsy lover. After hearing a little about his behavior, I had to agree, but I inquired about her response to him. She said, "I am always so turned off that I can barely stay in the same room with him." I wondered aloud whether he had been able to get any information about what she wanted. "We never talk about it," she said. I pointed out that a male is in a position of risk because he is often the initiator, and unless she communicated in some way what she preferred, he might feel so incompetent that he would make more, not fewer, mistakes. We discussed some possibilities for more open communication, but she refused, saying that it was improper for a woman to be openly suggestive about what she wanted. We talked about this for a while in an attempt to alleviate her guilty feelings. She finally agreed to try two or three of the more subtle suggestions I proposed. They were so subtle that I was afraid a person would need ESP to discern them. Her husband evidently had enough awareness, though, for when I saw her again, she said he had become a better lover. She shyly revealed that they might even talk about it one day.

Talking about what we expect from our spouses frees us from only some marriage problems. Unfortunately many of us marry with false expectations, one of the most common being the notion that our spouses are, and should be, the cause of our happiness. We therefore blame our partners unjustly for any unhappiness and feel perfectly justified in criticizing, blaming, or suggesting improvements. This whole notion, if not corrected, can cause a miserable life. When a wife, for example, depends on her husband for happiness, her husband will often conclude that he is being controlled and will begin to resist her attempts. This unleashes a whole cycle of strategies to improve the partner and counterstrategies to resist improving.

For instance, men will often try to communicate that they want more frequent and more passionate sexual responses from their wives. This message can be sent in hints—tales of other women's uninhibited desires for their husbands, gifts of suggestive lingerie, performance of favors (with strings attached)—or even in blatant demands for certain behavior. On the other hand, women will often want more emotional intimacy and warmth than their husbands ordinarily offer. A wife may think, with some justification, that she cannot be more passionate unless she first has intimacy. A husband may want to achieve intimacy through sex. The resulting strategies, resistance, and counter-strategies can become so elaborate as to be humorous. One man realized that the sparring had gone too far when the simple act of helping his wife set the table for dinner made her suspect he was trying to obligate her. "Oh, no, you don't!" she defiantly announced. "I know what you're after, and it won't work." This whole situation can be averted when couples talk about "what I want to be" in addition to "what I want from you."

As mature persons, we have gradually developed a set of ideas or principles about how we want to live regardless of how we are treated by someone else. In my case, being able to express my affection and warmth to my wife is very important. I learned that no matter how well my wife treated me, I could not be fully content or satisfied until I had acted consistently with "what I wanted to be." To create clear and accurate communication, both husband and wife need to formulate clear sets of ideas about their preferred way of acting and to communicate those to one another. This means that each must learn about "what I want to be" in as many shared marital situations as possible.

Most unhappy people are so involved in their marital struggle that they fail to recognize what they truly want for themselves and that they are responsible for their own happiness. When confronted with these ideas, most people see how reasonable they are. Some, at first, think the ideas seem selfish, but they are selfish only if we are exploiting our partner. A man I know sent his wife some flowers. For the rest of the day he felt uplifted, knowing that on the following day his wife would receive something to make her happy. It occurred to him that his feelings were improved even before his wife knew about the flowers. After she received them and said, "Thank you for the flowers you sent," he responded, "The flowers are for you, but the sending of them is for me." This man correctly understood that a good portion of his happiness was created by his own actions and not by how his wife treated him.

This sharing skill—talking about what we want from our partners and what we prefer for ourselves, and then listening for the same from our partners—can be easily applied to a sexual relationship. Both husband and wife can talk about a range of topics that may include an actual sexual encounter, the relationship of physical contact and affection, the conditions in which sexual activity best takes place, and the results each wants from participation in giving and receiving. This all sounds good, but can it work when conflict about sex has been long-standing? Yes. Unless there are physical problems that contribute to the difficulty, the solution to a troubled sexual relationship must be found in communicating and in making adjustments. Here, as with other marital problems, the first two steps will always be to do what is necessary to understand what each wants from the other and what each one wants to be.

HOW TO TALK—HOW TO LISTEN

Someone once said to me that more than ten thousand different messages can be transmitted between two conversing human beings in a five-minute span. I thought this number was excessive until I made a point of watching couples engage in fairly intense conversations. I observed messages such as voice tone, eye blinks, rate of talking, body posture, vocal hesitations, and word selection. I knew then that ten thousand was probably too conservative an estimate. I point this out to emphasize that in any attempt at communication, a good deal more information is sent than anyone will ever be able to comprehend. The best listeners are people who can get as much information as possible, paying attention to facial expressions, body movement, intensity of feelings, and who try to comprehend the speaker's motives. The best talkers are those whose speech and other messages are consistent and accurate in portraying the talker's intention. And, as I have said before, talking tends to become more accurate as listening skills improve.

When a husband and wife are unhappy, both tend to be suspicious and wary of one another. Without realizing it, they tend, in their listening and perceiving, to identify the words and actions they think will hurt them most. It is like a general who decides to spend his time on the beach watching for incoming bombers because his troops have been previously bombed by the enemy, and he wants to minimize further damage. Were we seeking to protect ourselves from pain, this might seem like an appropriate solution, but actually it only perpetuates the problem by narrowing the range of attention to just those potentially hurtful acts.

A list of ineffective listening styles illustrates the focus fear and suspicion create:

> *Nonattending.* The person ignores messages he doesn't want to discuss. Example: Speaker—"Do you think the kids watch too much television?" Listener—"There's nothing wrong with watching sports."
>
> *Computing.* The person notices the logical facts of messages and ignores the underlying feelings and purpose of the speaker. Example: Speaker (wife who hopes for support and warmth)—"I've had it! I'm so tired of the children I can't stand it!" Listener (husband)—"Every woman with five children would rather do something else."
>
> *Defending.* A person assumes that any statement made is an attack from which he must defend himself. Example: Speaker (wife)—"We ought to talk about how we're spending our money." Listener (husband)—"You waste just as much as I do, so don't blame me."
>
> *History giver.* A person creates security by responding with historical facts, removing the focus from the present conversation. Example: Speaker (wife)—"I would like to have another baby." Speaker (husband)—"You say that every time you see someone with a new baby."
>
> *Evidence user.* A person fears being wrong, so he supports each response with evidence. Example: Speaker—"I want to go out at least once a week." Listener—"No one goes out that often. Besides, what would we do without enough money to have fun?"

The *first step* in listening correctly is to expand the amount of information we receive. This means to use more inquiries that begin with such phrases as "I wonder if you could tell me...," "I'm interested in knowing...," or "I would appreciate it if you could explain to me...." If we use these and then just ask more questions for general information, avoiding sensitive areas, we can lengthen the time between our negative reactions and reduce the emotional intensity of any conversation.

That is easy to explain why. When listeners are fearful, not only do they focus just on what they are willing to pay attention to, but they also attempt, at the first sound of something that seems harmful, to protect themselves by shutting off the speaker's comments. The speaker typically interprets this not as a self-protective device but as an attack, and responds defensively. A listener's responsibility is to forestall development of this self-protective and fearful cycle by responding in a noncommittal way, but with attention to and interest in what the speaker has to say. This first step promotes a safe environment for the speaker and reduces tension.

The *second step* in listening is based on the idea that any message sent is actually three messages: (1) the meaning of the words spoken, (2) the reactions the sender wants from the listener, and (3) the underlying feelings associated with the message. All communication occurs at these three levels simultaneously. A good listener will be able to interpret all three and identify which is the most important to the sender at the time.

In the happiest marital relationships, couples simply respond first with an understanding of the literal meaning of the words. They then use this interpretation to understand what they should do and how the speaker feels. However, during conflict, miscommunication can occur at any or all three levels. Couples may misinterpret the meaning of the words, they may fail to understand what actions are desired, and they may be insensitive to or inaccurately perceive how the speaker feels.

If the meaning of the words is unclear, the listener can concentrate instead on the third message—understanding the underlying feelings. Most people think that their own feelings are more important than anyone else's and appreciate any effort by others to understand their feelings. Periodically asking if the speaker is feeling unhappy, lonely, frustrated (or some other emotion) can reduce the speaker's anxieties and allow him to focus better on what he is saying.

Table 2
Three Messages

1. Understanding the meaning of the words	Usually this is the first message acknowledged by the listener. This is accomplished when the listener says, "I understand you to say that . . ." or "Are you saying that . . .?" These listening responses and any others like them help the speaker feel safe in saying what he or she is thinking.
2. Understanding the reactions the speaker wants	An important part of listening is learning what needs to be accomplished. After the words are correctly understood, then understanding the speaker's desired reaction is important. This is accomplished by saying, "What do you want me to do . . .?" or "It seems like I should . . . Is that right?"
3. Understanding the underlying emotions	Acknowledging understanding of feelings is good anytime, but it is especially good when the speaker is talking about a problem, when the speaker is upset, or when the speaker is disclosing personal information. This acknowledgment is made by correctly showing understanding of the speaker's feelings—"I can see you're happy"—or by asking "What do you feel . . .?" Then emotions must be adjusted to respond appropriately to the speaker's emotions (i.e., warmth for warmth, sympathy for anger, and so on).

Suppose a couple has been arguing over some aspect of their sexual relationship—for example, the husband's tendency to initiate sexual relations without regard for the emotional context in which they occur. Perhaps the stress or frustration in his own life has raised the need for a strong emotional response from his wife. From her perspective, she may feel that they have been together a great deal but that there has been little affection expressed between them. She may see herself simply as the person who must give her husband an emotional release. This, in her mind, places her in a highly unfavorable situation.

Before this situation can be resolved, the husband must feel that his wife understands the emotional background for his request for sexual involvement and the emotional outcome he is seeking. Furthermore, the husband must be able to understand the emotions of his wife, who believes that some of her emotional needs are being neglected and perhaps even abused because he seems insensitive to them. In my experience, no successful solution is ever found unless the two can first understand the emotions involved. The solution depends on the couple's ability to say that they can feel and understand each other's emotions. Then they can usually make the modest adjustments that allow them to answer their partner's emotional needs.

The *third step* in listening stems from the position a listener is in. If a speaker has sent a message and a listener has received it, the listener must decide on a response. This response can greatly increase the effectiveness of the communication. Simple statements such as "I appreciate knowing that," or "I'm really glad you've told me," or "It's nice to know how you're feeling about this matter" are effective ways of using praise as a response to the speaker's statement. Much, of course, has been written about the use of positive responses, but the simple truth remains that there is seldom enough praise in any marriage relationship, and its importance to happiness cannot be overestimated.

Some people may wonder how they could think of anything nice to say when they're angry at their spouses. I would suggest that there never is a time when something in their spouse cannot evoke in them a positive response. The listener simply has to look for it. Taking the time to look is a small price to pay for marital happiness.

I saw the dramatic effects of this one day when a wife, quite justifiably, vented her anger at her husband. Her tirade went on for two or three minutes while he sat listening, not reacting to anything she said. Her statements had been fairly angry, even cruel. Instead of responding similarly, he smiled a bit and said, "Although I don't agree with everything you've said, I want you to know I really appreciate what you've said, and I know you wouldn't have said it unless you cared about our marriage." His statement took the wind out of her sails, and diminished her anger. She then acknowledged that her frustrations had been somewhat exaggerated but were still basically as she had expressed them. He acknowledged the need for some adjustment on his part, and a resolution was made within a few minutes. This problem had been building in pressure for some weeks, but they resolved it easily. A person with lesser confidence would have responded to anger with anger, and the couple would have been further from a solution.

TALKING AND LISTENING: HOW TO BEGIN

We can begin to develop the basic sharing skills of talking and listening by following a simple outline. This outline presents a sequence that is useful in sharing an experience without argument.

1. Choosing one issue. We begin by identifying one single, small issue and agreeing to talk about it and nothing else until we have told "what I want to be" and "what I want from you." Often couples bring several issues at one time into a discussion, which prevents any successful conclusions. When this happens, we become more convinced that we cannot share peacefully with each other.

2. Using nonthreatening language. In speaking, we should often mingle two messages: (1) why we care about the relationship and (2) what we think about the topic at hand. Fearful people believe that their relationships may be of little value to their partners, and they are reassured to hear explicit statements that their spouses do, in fact, care. When we speak, we should also indicate that we are talking because we do care. At the same time, we must, as clearly as possible, express what we think about a given topic in a nonthreatening way. This can be done by emphasizing "I" language, that is, the speaker must say such things as "This is my opinion," or "I think...," or "This is something that's been on my mind," without using a great deal of evidence and without condemning.

3. Summarizing. When we listen, we should summarize or repeat the meaning of the speaker's statement and identify the

speaker's emotions, doing so until the speaker feels understood and acknowledges it. Summarizing is an important aspect of listening: it demonstrates that we are sensitive to our spouses' ideas and feelings and indicates an interest in knowing.

4. Changing roles. Once the listener has understood the speaker, the roles change. The new speaker sends a message to be heard and accepted without agreement, disagreement, or any attempt at solution. We must keep in mind here that the goal is not necessarily to make a decision (unless one must be made right away). The objective is simply to talk about one thing without arguing. Once we have accomplished this two or three times, then we have increased confidence in our ability to talk and listen to each other peacefully.

All human beings benefit from the knowledge that someone understands them. This is especially true in an emotionally laden relationship like marriage. A sensitive listener who can pay attention to the emotional aspects of a message does much to help the speaker show kindness and speak clearly.

Any couple who wants a more productive marriage can begin by improving the sharing skills of talking and listening. All they need is a willingness to allow both to participate. It is wise, I believe, to view learning to talk and to listen as learning to dance. Talking and listening is the artful dance of communication. It is an ebb and a flow, a giving and a receiving, a speaking and an understanding that eventually create a bond of trust, a firm foundation for marital happiness.

3

SHOWING COMMITMENT

People in love are often surprised at the intensity of their feelings. Many fear this intensity and feel susceptible to the other person's influence. Yet, as couples marry and share conversation, sexual intimacy, childbirth, and financial problems, a deep bond is forming that commits each to the other. This bonding is natural and unavoidable, and as long as both are committed to the relationship, it will be positive and satisfying. However, if one or both spouses distance themselves from each other, conflict and alienation will result. A bond will still be created, but it will be weak, and the commitment will take a negative form.

Negative commitment can be identified quite easily. Usually, expressions of affection are absent or infrequent. Rather than live in a climate of total indifference, either party will occasionally say or do something that strikes a note of painful response in the other. The resulting reaction, even though negative, is an indication that one can still influence or affect the other. This achieves a perverse form of satisfaction.

Negative commitment can sometimes affect physical well-being. Many lonely and uncared-for wives and husbands have developed symptoms of physical illness, the most common being headaches, depression, back pain, or a general flu-like malaise. In many cases the stress and pain of noninvolvement results in actual physical disability. The physical illness causes the companion to pay attention.

An example of this can be found in the marriage of one busy professional. His work appeared to require excessive amounts of his time. Since he held a position of importance in his company, he had a telephone pager attached to his belt so that he could respond at any time. The result, of course, was that his wife felt neglected and saw herself as unimportant to him. She attempted to compensate by developing activities of her own. She joined some civic groups, participated in her church activities, and devoted increased amounts of time to her children. Then she strained her back quite severely in a minor automobile accident.

Since she was now required to rest in bed, her husband rearranged his work schedule so that he could attend to her at home and take care of their children. The attention she received and the commitment she felt from him made her much happier than she had been before. As time passed, she was unable to recover as rapidly as her physician expected. She also had relapses for no apparent reason. Finally her physician told her and her husband that there was no longer any medical basis for her back problem. She insisted that the physician must be mistaken and went to another clinic. They also found no physical problem, but they gave her some medication anyway.

When her husband complained that his work was suffering, she argued that some problem must still exist or she would not have to take the medication. This pattern continued for many years. She visited numerous clinics, but in each case she was unable to resolve her back problem completely. I wonder what would have happened to these two people had they been willing and able to organize their lives to evidence a strong and positive commitment without one of them feeling the need to be disabled.

Perhaps the most negative forms of commitment are the use of threats and the tactic of withdrawal from the relationship. Quite frequently, during an argument, one or both partners will threaten to leave the marriage. Although the couple will not follow through on these threats at first, eventually one spouse will test the commitment of the other by threatening to withdraw immediately. This approach assumes that, if one threatens and acts as if he will leave, the other will protest and say something like "No, please don't go! I can't stand being away from you." Such threats, however, are more often met by angry rejection, so that, instead of the desired result of increased commitment, the actual result is separation of some kind. Many divorces have occurred simply because, having threatened to separate, one person feels compelled to carry out the threats to avoid giving in or losing face or pride.

The most common form of negative commitment is found in the use of power. One or both spouses, fearing the other is not committed, can demand evidence of commitment. One woman I know used love tests. When feeling neglected, she would ask her husband to do a few things for her. On one occasion she asked him to change the blown-out light in the hallway. He was busy, and assuming that it was a minor chore, he neglected to do it for three or four days. At the end of that time she erupted, announcing angrily that he certainly must not love her very much—otherwise he would not have ignored her request. There were many other, more creative tests of love she gave him. She often insisted that a loving husband would help with the dishes or other housework. A loving husband, she said, was willing to spend time with his wife in activities outside the home. Many of her love tests were conducted in such secrecy that her husband was not aware of them. If she told him, how could they be a true test of his commitment? As a result, he failed most of them. When he failed a love test, she would write a note suggesting that a loving and committed husband would sacrifice his own life in one way or another to satisfy his wife. She would probably not have engaged in love tests had she been more secure and, more importantly, had her husband shown his commitment more openly.

All of the foregoing are ways in which couples show negative commitment. Insecurity, the fear of one or both spouses that they are not loved—these result in acts of negative commitment. Ironically, it would take considerably less energy to simply show positive commitment. Many people live entire lives seeking to obtain commitment through negative means, not realizing that their time is being filled with anxiety instead of affection. No couple can fill their marriage with negative acts and hope to achieve the marriage relationship they desire.

COMMITMENT AND FREEDOM

The first step in developing skill in positive commitment is to recognize that every person wants a certain amount of freedom along with companionship. Freedom here means the opportunity to choose and act on one's choice. Restricting a spouse's freedom will curtail the growth of commitment, as the following list of ways to diminish freedom illustrates:

Interruptions. A person who interrupts demonstrates disregard for another person's words and opinion. Frequent interruptions form the impression that the interrupted person's viewpoint is not reliable.

Accusations and blame. Accusations focus on negative behavior and invite defensiveness. Fear of being wrong or of losing the argument restricts one's sense of freedom. Blame places the responsibility on another's shoulders and involves a refusal to accept responsibility for one's own actions.

Disregard. When a person disregards another, keeping his thoughts and decisions to himself, he creates suspicion and allows for misinterpretation.

Explosive anger. Anger intimidates; it creates fear and dependence. Since anger attempts to overpower the person to whom it's directed, spouses should pay attention to their angry partners with caution.

Overconcern. When a partner worries excessively about the other, he asks questions or expects certain behavior, both of which apply pressure.

Overconformity. Some people develop an excessive obligation to conform to customs and rules. This appears in perfectionism, guilt, and dependence on some form of authority.

Immaturity. A person shows immaturity when he consistently resists proper authority or custom, is often indecisive, and frequently acts impatient. Since these characteristics cannot be ignored, immaturity forces a person to respond.

These seven kinds of behavior all limit freedom in some way by attempting to control the spouse's behavior and limiting one's own actions. They also weaken the bonds in marriage and are forms of negative commitment. Interestingly, the only way we can find out if our partners are truly committed is by allowing them freedom. If a person is free, without constraint, then any acts of commitment he does are truly as they appear. In contrast, the same acts done under some form of pressure are probably the result of acquiescence than of commitment. In order for true commitment to be expressed and to grow, freedom must exist within the marriage.

Freedom in marriage can be enhanced in two important ways. First is to restrict the number of limiting actions, particularly those on the preceding list. Second is to willingly increase one's acts of commitment without expecting any response from the other. One person acting in a constructive way, on a sustained basis, can alone increase the amount of freedom because the marriage benefits from greater stability and calm.

When we consistently act according to our own choice, we will learn that the responsibility for our behavior lies within ourselves and that our behavior does not have to be determined by pressure from another. Of course, we can all think of times when we have tried to be nice to someone who did not reciprocate. Some of us may have concluded that in marriage one person cannot improve the situation if the other is not willing to participate. This is true, I believe, in some instances. Much more often, however, one person's sustained acts of love and commitment will have enormous power, regardless of the spouse's response.

If one person has treated a marriage partner considerately for a period of time and has experienced little improvement, setting up prearranged reciprocal bargains can be helpful. For example, if a wife wants her husband to spend more time with her, the husband could ask the wife for a reciprocal response—something he wants from her. Positive "bargains" like these are not only appropriate but exceptionally useful in helping each spouse feel more committed to the other. All a couple need to do is identify what each wants from the other and agree about exchanging fairly and equally. I will discuss this process later.

COMMITMENT AND SACRIFICE

Everyone fails to perform perfectly at one time or another. If a marriage is to be stable, one partner's failure will elicit understanding support from the other. Over a lifetime both spouses will be involved in giving support during failure or need, but oftentimes there is only one who is giving unselfishly. Such a person is sacrificing something of himself, an important act of commitment.

Sacrifice may be best understood in the life of Jesus Christ. This one person has engendered more commitment from people than anyone else. What is the cause of this extraordinary degree of commitment? I believe it is because he embodies the principle of and devoted his life to sacrifice, especially to a sacrifice that would allow us to obtain eternal life. He chose to act and perform, without coercion and at great cost to himself, a sacrifice not only of his life but of all his energy, time, and resources, and demanded no guaranteed reward for his sacrifice. He simply offered it to everyone but allowed each person freedom to choose whether he would use it. The combination of these conditions—acting without coercion, sacrificing self without a guaranteed reward—impels us to question in order to understand, to learn in order to be faithful, and to commit in order to express gratitude. These same conditions can be applied in the lives of married people with results that may not be as universal but are still as dramatic.

I have known a married couple who, for the greater part of their twent-year marriage, have lived without much expression of affection or commitment. Both worked hard on their respective duties in marriage, but neither was happy. Because of their religious values, divorce did not appear to be a suitable solution to their unhappiness. The alternative, remaining in such a sterile, unhappy marriage, finally overtook them, and they sought ways to resolve their discord. Neither had experienced much of the positive side of life in their childhood. Both tended to be critical, emotionally distant, and unable to express much love. For example, on birthdays one person would remember the birthday and give the other a gift, but the other would typically fail to acknowledge the gift, and then an argument would ensue. Although they had had many discussions about their problems, neither seemed willing to change.

Finally, more out of desperation than anything else, the woman decided that she would be willing to begin sacrificing for her marriage. She decided that she would try to express fondness and care for her husband by traditional acts of commitment —giving gifts, paying compliments, and serving in one way or another. Eventually she attempted more elaborate acts of commitment—inviting her husband to spend a weekend with her in a hotel, for instance. During the weeks that followed she occasionally became very discouraged. Nothing she did seemed to affect her husband's behavior, and she often wept lonely, hopeless, and bitter tears. When she told me about her efforts, I explained that, if she chose to persist, she must do so without expecting her husband to change. She responded, "Then what good is it to do what I'm doing?" I asked her if she felt better about herself. Her response was that she did. She said that she had "come alive" and felt happier about herself than she had for many years. I then said, "You can see at least one benefit from acting in a committed fashion. Your husband has lived the way he has lived for many years, and you would not expect him to undergo a dramatic change simply from a few weeks of your positive example. You must realize that your husband is not one who knows how to act committed and that he's choosing not to learn. He simply does not know how to express himself as a committed man to a woman."

She was not content to let my statements go unsupported and asked for evidence. I pointed to his early background and to his actions in the marriage and asked her if she had ever known him to act in a loving way on a sustained basis with her. She thought for a moment and replied that he gave her some additional money when asked. He had never been able to demonstrate, except sporadically, acts of love and care for her.

Their situation continued as it was for some time, with some ups and downs. Finally, when she gained enough strength and learned to sacrifice without expecting any response of commitment from her husband, she began to feel calmer and happier about her marriage. Ironically, that was the time her husband confessed that he recognized his ineptness as a husband and, although he had much to learn, began a process of showing his commitment to her more openly. I do not mean to suggest that this couple changed dramatically and went, within a matter of days or weeks, from unhappiness to sheer happiness. They have, even now, much more progress to make, but they have begun to see the rewards already: they argue less frequently, they know fewer painful experiences, and when negativc interaction happens, it does not last as long as before.

This improvement resulted from the consistency of one partner. Since the wife applied no pressure to act in a prescribed way, the husband could choose to show or to not show commitment. Further, she expected no guarantee that their life would be different. Her sacrifice and commitment and the atmosphere of freedom altered their lives significantly for the better.

I am not suggesting that this will always be the result. But I am proposing that when one partner does not do his or her part, the other must face a decision: to get angry and frustrated or to offer a loving sacrifice. When we are mature enough to choose sacrifice, we are unmistakably demonstrating our commitment to our marriage.

COMMITMENT AND PARENTS

Most of us find that we marry a family as well as a spouse. We are fortunate if the relationship with parents is harmonious, less so if the relationship is difficult. Sometimes one or both spouses cannot make the emotional separation from parents. At times the parents cannot let go, intruding on the married couple through frequent visits, too much advice or too much financial help, or too much involvement in marital problems. It can be worse if married children are tied to a family business.

Another common problem with parents stems from one spouse speaking negatively about the other to the parents and then telling the offended spouse the parental reaction. Personality differences can also cause awkwardness between in-laws and spouses. Sometimes the couple and their in-laws will avoid each other, but this too may lead to even more difficulty.

The most common cause of in-law problems, however, is a failure to recognize that, because of marriage, parents and children both are facing new ways of doing things. A son- or daughter-in-law is faced with the spouse's family style and traditions. Instead of just one marriage relationship to organize, they must find a place for relationships with two other families—a complex task that some fail to master.

In-law relationships can be organized happily if we use the skills of sharing. This means, ideally, that before negative conditions arise, we begin to create a positive bond. The table on the following page shows the kinds of situations a couple may face with their in-laws and suggests a few steps to improve relationships between them.

The process of commitment sometimes seems to be juggled between devotion to our marriage and time, attention, and emotional involvement with our parents. Generally it is wise to emphasize marital commitment before and during any contact with parents. Doing this for a while will eventually assure our spouses of our priorities and help them be pleased about in-law relationships.

One couple went to the same high school and grew up a few miles from each other. After marriage they attended a university in a neighboring state. When they visited their home town they received invitations from both sets of parents and felt obligated to spend equal time at each place. This led to two Thanksgiving dinners, two Christmas celebrations, and to complex scheduling. The frustration created arguments between them, and they argued nearly every time they visited their parents. On one occasion as they were traveling toward their parents' homes, they discussed the problem and found that both had similar feelings: they wanted to please their parents and felt guilty if they failed. They decided to do what they themselves wanted to do, sometimes being together in one home and sometimes separating. They both had to tell their respective parents "no" on occasion, but their visits became much more pleasant.

Table 3
In-laws and Commitment

Situation	Improvement
Your spouse has loving relationships with his or her parents	Easiest situation to share. Improve good experiences by communicating positive things about your in-laws to your spouse and about your spouse to your in-laws. Participate in some important traditional family activities.
Your spouse has difficulty relating to his or her parents	Make separation complete by emphasizing your marriage, screening out conflict with in-laws. The solution is to mutually agree on a style of relating to (or avoiding) your in-laws. Show support of the spouse to the parents, but don't be active in conflict.
Your spouse has relatives who intrude and try to control your family	Use the most appropriate strategy: (1) Confront the issue openly. The spouse who is the child must do this. (2) Modify behavior where necessary. A couple may be inadvertently allowing parental involvement through their indecisiveness or disorganization. (3) Avoid complaining to your spouse or criticizing his or her family. Work out ways to reduce communication with in-laws except on your terms.
Your spouse keeps too close an emotional bond with his or her parents	Since this prevents marital sharing, calmly discuss the situation and ask for adjustments. Don't talk to your in-laws about your marriage. If no change occurs, seek professional help as quickly as possible. This kind of problem can persist for a long time.
You have difficulty relating to your in-laws	Use the most appropriate strategy: (1) Agree to disagree, and allow your spouse to have a good relationship with his or her parents, even if you don't participate. (2) Join in short-term family activities to get to know each other better. Some problems are from poor communication. (3) Encourage your spouse to give positive feedback about you to your in-laws.

This example illustrates how every marriage must be protected by the two people in it. Even though their parents were being considerate and were not trying to exert control, the emotional ties both felt to their parents led to too much effort to please them and to too little concern for their own relationship. Their recommitment to their union resolved the problem, but it required that they both communicate to their parents where their true loyalties lay. Having done this, they were happier.

Most of us can have good marriages and maintain good relationships with our parents and in-laws. It requires a balance between priority to the marriage and regard for our relatives. When this condition is created, marriage is shared positively, and our circle of happiness is enlarged.

4

RECEIVING LOVE

Love and marriage have been tied so closely together in song and literature that we usually cannot think of one without the other. Whatever love comes to mean as we mature, we assume that marriage is going to provide it. For some of us, however, these expectations are not met. Often, this is not because marriage itself could not provide a loving environment, but because married individuals find some way to diminish love. The most common reason for the diminishment of love in marriage is that one or both spouses feel insecure and fail to admit or accept the love in their marriage as authentic. In other words, those who cannot find love in their marriages may accuse their partners of not loving them but instead are often merely incapable of recognizing love when they see it or of accepting it when it is given. Those same people may fear expressing their own love to their partners because they do not wish to be obligated, to be vulnerable to someone who might not love in return. All who cannot receive love, who fail to notice it, or who refuse to accept its obligations will diminish it.

So, while most people want love, many fear it as well, or at least find their desire to be loved accompanied by so much anxiety that they cannot calmly and securely receive love. For some reason, believing that we are loved requires that we rely on someone else's ability to express it to us. This can be terrifying to some people. Fear of such vulnerability can be great enough to cause these people to deny love.

The causes of this fear stem from previous social experiences, usually ones that occurred during childhood and that involved suffering. A woman I know was reared in a family where abuse was common. Neither of her parents was very good at loving. She told me of her father's explosive temper. She said she never knew when he would erupt into anger and vent his hostility on her. Furthermore, her father was given to periods of depression often lasting for several days. During such periods he withdrew emotionally from his wife and children. Even in the best of times, he was not given to much demonstration of affection or warmth. He frequently argued with his children, and as they matured he became increasingly sarcastic and bitter in his arguments. His wife was a quiet, compliant person, cowed by his explosiveness. She failed to establish a bond of warmth with this daughter, who grew up believing that her mother did not love her.

As a child, my friend adapted to these circumstances by using her intellect: she developed a strong sense of competition characterized by zealous use of logic. Her preoccupation with rational thought excluded intuition or reliance on emotion. Her intense motivation to achieve hid her mistrust of other people. She *could* receive praise for her achievements and her excellent organizational ability. In fact, later she became known as a capable and efficient woman who occupied many positions of leadership in church and community. She could not receive affection, though. When her husband said or did anything loving, she was unresponsive, often speechless. In fact, she would fly in the face of the obvious and frequently conjure up from her husband's mistakes evidence that he didn't care about her.

When I met him I immediately saw his frustration. He was a kind and demonstrative man who was truly in love with his wife. She was an attractive, talented woman. Although she had an intellectual appreciation for the need to be loving and could be superficially affectionate, she could not easily receive the affection of others, nor would she allow herself to feel any strong feelings toward them. Her fear had created an emotional desert in her. It was painful to watch how she would refuse to face the possibility that her husband's love was genuine. Without realizing why, she would magnify his small foibles into faults, causing conflict that would distance herself from her husband's affection. Many times she accused him of neglect, only to retreat from her position when confronted with his version of the facts.

On some level, of course, this woman wanted a loving marriage. It was obvious from her choice of a mate. She also wanted to be able to express love openly and freely to her husband and children. However, all attempts she made to improve her ability to accept and express love increased her apprehension. This resulted in a frustrating cycle—she would invest small amounts of love, only to follow them with increased periods of distance and isolation.

I wish this woman's experience were uncommon. Unfortunately, it is not. Many people seek marriage in order to find the love that eluded them as children, failing to realize that inexperience is a poor teacher. We cannot express or receive what we have had no chance to feel and know. Since a successful marriage requires higher levels of giving and receiving love than any other relationship, these people, naive and unprepared, enter a relationship that intensifies their fears and increases their unhappiness.

There are other reasons besides insecurity and fear for the failure to believe in a companion's love. A significant one is guilt. This may come from sexual abuse by some inconsiderate and irresponsible person. Even though sexually abused people have been dominated by people more powerful than they, such people typically feel as if they should bear part of the shame and guilt. Of course, nothing could be further from the truth. Sexually abusive events are so traumatic that disturbed feelings result, feelings so strange that they cannot be explained; and this confusion perpetuates the memory of them.

Equally unfortunate are the results of sexual promiscuity. I have known many people who, prior to marriage, established sexual relations with several partners. At the time they felt that sharing sex was simply a means to establish a sense of closeness, to strengthen a relationship with another person. But the truth is that for every temporary bond there is a distance and isolation that follows. In effect, sexual activity prior to marriage is a form of emotional alienation that increases the likelihood that one will fear a close relationship.

People whose pasts are cluttered with promiscuous kinds of experiences will often find their ability to love and to be loved in marriage impaired. These often become people who, in their anxiety, frequently create love tests for their companions. But, as we saw earlier (in chapter three), love tests don't work. Any behavior motivated by anxiety actually creates conditions that can prevent a person from having his emotional needs fulfilled. Oddly enough, people who are afraid of not being loved actually engage in behavior that prevents someone from loving them. This behavior can take several forms:

> *Denial.* A person makes statements about not being loved. Very often associated with feelings of inferiority, such statements are an indirect invitation for the spouse to say, "But I *do* love you." A spouse's proclamation of love is rejected by further denial, "Oh, no, you don't."
>
> *Accusation.* A person accuses a spouse of not being loving. A person picks out negative incidents and uses them as evidence, meanwhile ignoring loving gestures.
>
> *Refusal.* A person does not respond to attempts that communicate love. If a gift is given, for example, the person demonstrates only perfunctory appreciation. Many attempts are wholly ignored.
>
> *Love tests.* A person sets up a task or decides on certain ways a spouse should act to "prove" his or her love. Sometimes an unsuspecting spouse inadvertently "passes the test," which leads the insecure spouse to develop another test.
>
> *Pouting and sulking.* A person sullenly withdraws, which is supposed to invite demonstrations of love; or the "unloved" person acts in a way that implies he or she is not loved. If the pouting person at first refuses the loving response and then relents, the stage is set for a rerun, and a cycle of negative behavior begins.

If happiness in marriage depends, at least in part, on how abundant the loving experiences are, we must conclude that a satisfying marriage requires that partners overcome their fear of being loved. Because the rewards are so great, we might think that this would be easy, but if someone has been victim to abuse or neglect, that person tends to believe an absence of love constitutes part of reality. When this belief has been confirmed by repeated experiences, changing this conviction is as difficult as modifying any other part of a personality. I have seen people literally tremble at the prospect of accepting the idea that someone loves them. Feeling love toward their mates is all right, but believing they were loved in return was something beyond their abilities.

SOCIAL EXPERIENCES AND RECEIVING LOVE

Those who fail to receive love are often participants in unsatisfactory social experiences, which leads to frustration or discomfort as a married couple attempt to organize their social life with friends and neighbors. Sometimes one person, feeling confident, will seek the companionship of others only to find that the spouse neither likes these friends nor wants their company. The result is that one person has a satisfactory social life and the other does not, or neither has much of a social existence, or they pursue their social experiences separately. Failure to share positively in a balanced social life impairs marital intimacy.

In attempting to resolve fear, we must assume that the hurt caused by humans can in part be cured by humans. This means that, to overcome the fear of being loved, we must incorporate positive social experiences into our plan. Furthermore, if we are married, experiencing these social experiences as a couple is important because a shared experience benefits the marriage relationship more than a positive experience had by only one of the partners. This is not to say that a spouse should not experience individual social rewards. I am merely suggesting that, in a relationship where one or both partners fear love, seeking out more positive shared social experiences can help.

One couple had been invited to join a mixed bowling team organized by the husband's work associates. They had turned down the invitation several times, but at my insistence they reluctantly joined and bought their shirts and some equipment. On the first night of their league game, they neither helped the team greatly nor hindered it, but they met their goal, which was to learn the names of all the people on the team. They felt at least more comfortable at the end of the evening than at the beginning. On a subsequent night they helped the team by scoring higher than the team average. As they told me of this experience, I asked if anyone had praised them or shown appreciation. The wife said that she had received several compliments, but the husband said he couldn't remember any. This was not surprising to me, since he had had an unhappy early life. When his wife pointed out that several team members had complimented him, only then was he able to remember.

As we discussed this incident, the husband considered the possibility that other people at work, at church, or in community groups had responded to him positively. He was, however, largely unprepared or unwilling to accept their appreciation. I asked him to identify, in the next few days, how many times he failed to acknowledge other people's positive responses. I was interested in helping him recognize that there were helpful people in his life. After several days he returned to say that he had failed to acknowledge encouragement from others on four or five occasions.

His next assignment was to emphasize his denial, actively disqualifying or ignoring people's attempts to express affection and warmth to him. On the second day after our conversation he telephoned to ask if he could discontinue this assignment. He said that he had become more fully aware of what he had been doing his whole life and that he had rejected the positive gestures of people who he thought disapproved of him. His final remark has always stayed in my mind: "I have been the one who has refused to love by refusing to let people love me."

This man and his wife sought out an increased number of social opportunities. They found a few close friends and joined a church group. They found that increased social activity enabled them to feel better about themselves and helped them to communicate (that is, give and receive) affection in their marriage.

SOCIAL ACTIVITIES AND SELF-ESTEEM

The fear of being loved is closely related to low self-esteem. Anyone who feels a sense of inadequacy can easily disbelieve another person's love. Part of self-esteem is the amount of comfort and confidence we feel in social relationships. Therefore, as we use shared social experiences to overcome fears of being loved, we can reasonably expect that self-esteem will also improve.

Subtle communication failures can also result in low self-esteem. For example, downcast eyes or fragmented statements when talking to people can cause a person to miss communication cues from other people, which increases the probability of misunderstanding. When we either misperceive or send messages difficult to understand, social discomfort is heightened.

A friend of mine told me of a problem in his marriage that indicated he was a person who feared love. Although he had been married, apparently happily, for several years, he felt as though his wife didn't love him. There was little evidence that this was true, so he asked me how he could eliminate this fear. I noticed as he talked with me that his eyes were averted from mine. Other times while talking he would scrutinize my responses so intensely that he failed to express himself coherently.

I suggested to him that, for the next few days whenever he talked to someone, he should focus his attention on the person's Adam's apple. I told him that since a person cannot tell exactly where a listener's eyes are focused, he would appear to be noticing the speaker's face without having to actually do it. He agreed to try this for several days and report back.

He found that speaking to others when he didn't look at their faces was somewhat easier for him. I then suggested that he make up a story, any story, and tell it to his family or close friends. He was reluctant at first, but he finally agreed. When he returned a few days later, he said that he had found the courage to do it only three times, and all three of those were to his wife and children, whose responses were positive. He pressed me for the reason behind this request. I explained that we cannot tell a story of any kind, even one made up, that does not reveal something about ourselves. My intention was to get him to present some personal information in a disguised form (the made-up story) to other people. This way he could judge their responses to him without having to overtly reveal personal things about himself. Since the responses he had received were positive, he was willing to take the next step—actually telling others about himself and about his experiences. He learned that they responded positively to those experiences as well.

This raises a crucial point. Anyone seeking to improve his or her social experiences must recognize that social warmth is contingent on the ability to speak about and to listen to personal information. When one person tells a personal experience to another who understands it, the understanding confirms the speaker's experience. This social confirmation is sought by all human beings.

So I next asked my friend to think of personal experiences that would be appropriate to share in various social situations. We identified some social settings at work, at home, and at his church, and we talked about a personal experience he could tell in each of these settings. He agreed to try this. When he reported back, the look on his face and the light in his eyes were evidence to me that he had found other people who were genuinely interested in him. He acknowledged that he noticed smiles, nods of understanding, and compliments in response to his ideas. He was on his way to overcoming his fear of receiving love from other people.

I would like to emphasize that I did not fabricate nice things to say to him to improve his self-esteem, nor did I attempt to demonstrate logically that his feelings were inappropriate. His gradual and modest attempts to invest in some social behavior brought the success. Everyone needs and benefits from good companionship. When we seek this out as individuals and couples, still keeping some private time for our marriage, the quality of our marriage relationship improves.

ACKNOWLEDGING LOVE

Merely by acknowledging love, we can increase the flow of it in marriage. When we say, "I feel loved by you," in words or actions, we increase the probability that more gestures of love will be forthcoming. There are many ways to acknowledge love, including expressing gratitude and resolving differences. Though the reconciliation of differences is not usually thought of as a way to acknowledge love, attempts to resolve differences, as the following list indicates, promote a positive social life and clearly send the messages "I love you" and "I feel loved by you."

Taking turns. A couple can take turns meeting each other's needs—a good way to resolve differences.

Finding variety. A couple can find some new activities and do them together every month or two.

Sharing an activity. A couple can plan an activity, such as a dinner party, and divide the responsibilities for preparation equally.

Declaring a truce. A couple can establish a rule that any social activity will be a time for a truce. Any criticisms (about being late, for example) and discussions of marital problems would be off limits during social activities.

Giving. A couple can plan social activities that involve giving small gifts, doing favors, or making extra efforts to please each other.

There is little in marriage more important than feeling successful at being loved. Knowing that we are loved builds self-esteem, and giving and receiving love creates intimacy. A person who is capable of receiving love from his or her spouse enriches their love and makes their marriage happier.

5

MAKING LOVE LAST

At first it seemed a bit unmanly to admit to myself that loving someone and being loved in return were the most important things in my life. One could judge from my actions that success in my career took priority in my life. But as I acquired more experience, I found that, although my work was satisfying, it did not create as much happiness for me as the time I spent with my wife and children. Though I was aware of this feeling, it still took some time before I could acknowledge that a lasting love was more important to me than anything else. I did not tell anyone for quite a while because I was still unsure of what others would think, but as time passed I became less shy about feeling it. I found out that loving another person was a gradual experience: I knew less about it at the beginning than I thought I did. My marriage has improved because I know more about love now, and the more I know, the more important it becomes to me.

I will always remember the moment I admitted to myself that loving my family was the most important of life's experiences. At that time I felt the panic and uncertainty the unskilled feel when faced with a task they do not know how to perform. I felt that I did not know how to love my wife or receive her love except in a superficial way.

I have known some people who can love only temporarily. They express love until they encounter some difficulty, and then their love is replaced by the disruption that follows. I don't want that for myself. I want a lasting love, one that exists even when difficulties arise. If husbands or wives fail to learn how to make love last, their marriages are likely to be unhappy. Love for them becomes a temporary condition; their marriages become a sporadic mix of love and other less desirable emotions.

TEMPORARY LOVE

There are many reasons that cause love between a husband and wife to become temporary rather than lasting. One of the worst is the attitude of external control. Briefly, people who are bound by notions of external control believe that what happens is always caused by someone or something outside themselves. They think that their unhappiness is a result of events or actions beyond their control. Thinking themselves innocent, they simply react to what is done to them.

When this belief is brought into marriage, the spouse is assigned responsibility for happiness. Such people conclude that if they are unhappy, their partners must be failing in some respect. Even if the unhappiness stems from some situation outside marriage, someone in the marriage will usually be partly blamed. This is also true for married people who believe that their partners' first responsibility is to please them. When they become dissatisfied with their marriages, they decide that their partners are responsible for their dissatisfaction.

The belief in external control unleashes a set of strategies instigated by one partner to make the other do what is desired, which are followed by counterstrategies to resist the loss of freedom. Marriages can become filled with strategies and resistance, counterstrategies and counterresistance. I have known couples whose marriage relationship is based totally on such interaction. Great instability is the result. As long as a spouse believes that the other spouse causes his problems and is responsible for his happiness, the couple's love will be temporary.

Another reason why love may be temporary can be found in childhood experiences, or rather in lack of experience. People who have learned to survive situations in which love is not often or openly expressed tend to attach importance to physical or concrete things. We call this "materialism." When such people are forced to choose between communicating some form of love and doing something that will gain possessions, they will more often choose the latter.

It is surprising, in light of the emphasis we all place on love, that temporary love is so widespread. Indeed, many place work before kindness and sensitivity; many place being "right" before understanding; and many live with pressures to succeed financially, cutting back on companionship with their families. We yield to social influence rather than show loyalty to our partners. We spend time pursuing new possessions rather than spend time showing love for each other. Then we wonder why our love is only part-time.

Equal in importance to the other reasons for temporary love is the third reason. Some adults have had unhappy experiences during dating and courtship years and believe they have been exploited by members of the other sex. If this attitude is present in marriage, it results in one person measuring the giving of love against the receiving of love. When a couple measure the love they give and receive, they limit its exchange because each is waiting for the other. This is selfish, and the measuring makes love occasional. People who love selfishly and immaturely try to enhance their own desires, and their selfishness becomes the parent of new exploitations of others. They thus establish a negative pattern in marriage that affects successive generations.

THE INVESTMENT

I have wondered what prevents us from expressing love. What risks do we face? Do we fear exploitation so much that we do not want to love more than our companions can or will? Why do we not instead realize that efforts on our part to increase the happiness of our partners will nearly always be returned, in most cases many times over our original investment?

The idea that love is reciprocal is often lost on those who measure the giving and receiving of love. Yet this reciprocity is basic to all aspects of love in married life. One couple had a lively disagreement about the type of Christmas tree they should buy. He liked full symmetrical trees, but she wanted fir trees with distinct branches. Their solution, as you might expect, was to alternate years, but she had difficulty finding a good specimen of the type of tree she preferred, so for two or three years the Christmas trees she selected were not very attractive. All of the children began to prefer the trees that daddy bought. One year, when it was his turn, he found a beautiful tree exactly like his wife would want. He bought it and took it home, putting it on the front porch. Later that evening he asked her if she wanted to look at his Christmas tree. When she saw it, she was astonished and said, "This is my tree!" He feigned puzzlement and, walking around the tree, replied, "How could that be? I've made a terrible mistake." She caught on and embraced him, touched by his concern. In the following days she spent much of her time thinking of ways to express her love to him.

This couple could tell us of the true nature of reciprocal giving. In most instances one partner merely needs to start the giving. When expressions of love include help for a companion, praise and approval, and warmth and affection, the result is nearly always much better than simply balancing the love you give with what you believe you have received.

RESPONSIBILITY TO DEVELOP LASTING LOVE

Lasting love, then, can be present only in marriages in which the partners are emotionally stable and can assume responsibility for their own feelings. Such people have a sense of inner control. They believe they can create positive feelings and, to some extent, eliminate negative feelings within themselves. They have learned responsibility by feeling a certain amount of freedom to make their own choices and by experiencing the consequences of their actions. When a couple allow each other to voice opinions and accept each other's opinions often, they create in marriage a climate of freedom that increases love. This kind of freedom is not license to do anything. It is simply a situation in which the husband and wife can participate openly and equally in making decisions.

Most people think that they are responsible, or at least not irresponsible, but many do not realize that they may be shirking much of the responsibility in marriage. One wife I know complained bitterly about the "pressure" she received from her husband. Yet, when asked about her goals for her marriage, she could not state what she wanted for herself in any area of marriage. Her husband complained that she was a reluctant sexual partner, that she was a disorganized housekeeper and mother, and that she was usually depressed. I suggested that, if she wished to stay married, she would have to decide what she wanted and get moving.

To my surprise, she hotly retorted, "I don't *have* to do anything!" Realizing that the anger she felt toward her husband masked her immaturity, I replied, "That's right—you don't have to do anything. You can walk out right now. You also never have to grow up. But if you fail to be responsible for yourself, you have no one to blame but yourself." She was crying by this time. I rose and left the room. She hurried out, and I thought I would not see her again. Two weeks later, I did. Her hand was outstretched as she said, "Thank you for waking me up."

My part was very small compared to her efforts. She described a week of depression, and then told how she had finally organized her home and work routine. She was obviously more confident as she talked about the ideas she had for her marriage. She had quite a ways to go, but she had begun to create her own freedom by assuming more responsibility for herself, expecting less and blaming less. She had begun to understand that she would experience an increase in love because of what she was willing to do.

Love is the companion of many other virtues, such as patience and gratitude. When we work to be more patient and to express gratitude more often and openly, we increase our ability to give and receive love. I have given assignments to people to spend one or two days practicing a positive trait. Merely by consciously focusing on one virtue, these people have improved the quality of their emotional lives. One woman who was practicing gratitude took the opportunity to write notes, to speak to people personally, and to do things for others as a way of expressing thankfulness. She said she had learned that gratitude pleased the receiver and ennobled the giver.

This emphasis on positive traits can sound maudlin to people who are accustomed to the realities of unhappiness; but to those who experience a great deal of love in their lives, the development of positive characteristics makes immediate sense. Those who have or wish to have lasting love will recognize the need for numerous positive character traits to sustain such a love.

Finally, a lasting love can only be maintained when people increase their variety in expressing it. Overt acts such as sending flowers and saying "I love you" are some of the most common. Just listening to someone's opinion, or helping when someone is tired, or being loyal when spouses are being criticized will also maintain love. One woman said she felt better about herself as she found new ways of expressing love to her husband. She said, "You will probably think this is trite, but I noticed that when we had guests for dinner I always served them first. One time I served my husband first and then the guests. As I walked by him, he reached up and squeezed my hand. I had not realized the significance of such small things." If we began to look for new ways to express love and could learn one or two methods a month, we would still find that throughout the many years of marriage we could not exhaust the possibilities.

CHILD CARE

There are, of course, unwanted children or "inconvenient" children, but a new human life born of a loving union is good evidence that a husband and wife's love for each other is meant to be lasting. The challenge is to find ways to remain in love while we go through the process of rearing our children.

Those who have children know that child care requires a consuming and complex effort and isn't always fun. It requires handling very strong emotions. Our feelings for our children are among the most intense feelings we will ever have. This intensity combined with the complexity of the task can create enough pressure to drive couples apart rather than bring them together.

About half of the married couples, by one spouse allowing the other a predominant role, avoid arguments. While this may reduce the number of arguments concerning the children, it increases resentment and frustration. Sharing the responsibilities is usually more effective—that means we commit ourselves to sharing evenly in the task of rearing our children, learn how to do it well, and then work to make it rewarding.

Understanding the most common reasons for not rearing children well will improve the quality of sharing in child care. One of these reasons, obviously, is that the amount of work involved in attending children is usually unequally divided. This happens most often when one parent is employed away from the home while the other is home taking care of the children. The more domestic parent may feel a great deal of frustration with the increasing pressures and demands of child rearing, especially when the other parent is away or has come home ready to rest from a "hard day at the office." Also, there is still the unfortunate residue of belief that child care is woman's work, and men, being less competent, should stay out of it.

There is much evidence, however, to show that fathers play a very significant part in child development. When both parents are not involved in child care, the children and the one uninvolved parent will surely miss some of life's best possible experiences.

Another common hindrance to happy child rearing lies in differing philosophies of child management. Married couples will usually encounter some differences due to their family backgrounds, beliefs, and personalities, and if they fail to work for harmony, the differences will persist, even increase. For example, if one parent is more indulgent than the other, the indulgent parent may see the strict parent as being unnecessarily harsh and may respond with increased warmth to balance the harshness. The stricter parent may then see the other parent's indulgence as being detrimental to the child's character, therefore compensating by being even firmer and stricter. Both become more extreme than they really want to be, and they share child care negatively because they have not found a compromise.

Husbands and wives who battle each other's management techniques fail to fully appreciate the consequences for the children. Most children will begin to use the situation to exploit their parents. They may also be inclined to learn deviant behavior because the parents, not being united, are often powerless to control how the child acts.

Differences in abilities can also obstruct effective parenting. If one parent is highly organized and desires to maintain a fairly regular routine while the other parent is fairly lax, their differences can prevent constructive child care. I once asked a couple to separately write down, without consulting each other, the rules they believed their children should follow. The husband handed me one piece of paper with six rules. The wife brought me four pieces of paper with single-spaced, typewritten rules covering each page. At first I could not believe she was serious. I soon realized, however, that part of their problem came from the fact that the mother had more rules than their children could possibly follow. Since the husband didn't share her attitude, he was unwilling to support her in her attempts to enforce the rules, and she was critical of his seeming indifference. Their family life, I might add, resembled a circus of angry people.

Yet another common difficulty between parents occurs when they have different notions about what they want their children to become. For instance, one parent may want a self-reliant, individualistic child, and so will try some form of "tough love." If the other parent wants a sensitive, compliant, conforming child, the strategy might be to envelop the child in warmth, protectiveness, and kindness. These objectives and methods could be coordinated, since both have value, even in cases where a couple feel no compromise is possible because they perceive their objectives to be so different. Of course, differences would also occur if one parent had clearly thought about desired characteristics for the children and if the other parent had not considered them much at all.

A serious pitfall in child rearing is the temptation to involve children in marital problems. This can happen in several ways. One is when one or both parents tell the child about the marital problems. What usually results is an inordinate sense of responsibility in the child that often prevents him or her from maturing healthily. A second way parents involve a child in marital conflict is to make the child the object of a marital message. An example of this could be when a husband, confronted with a wife who is not very affectionate, trains his daughter to be affectionate and on occasion mentions that he is happy his daughter is "warm and affectionate like a true woman should be"—obviously a message to the wife through the daughter.

Parents will also affect children through their marital problems. When married people spend energy in conflict about children, they often have little energy or interest left for the demanding tasks of child care. Marital conflict causes instability for the children and reduces the likelihood that parents will follow through on important child care responsibilities. Moreover, if children overhear conflicts, they may feel guilt, or they may fear that they are the cause of the pain. As children grow, they may begin to use marital conflict to manipulate their parents. As the children sense their parents' guilt, they can become very powerful in the home, more powerful than their parents. When they receive criticism, they can point out how imperfect their parents are. Through verbal abuse or other emotional ploys, they can demand that parents do what the children want. I have seen this tragic reversal of parent and child roles in an amazingly large number of families.

Couples should recognize that one of the most common difficulties in child care lies in the incompetence and/or ignorance of one or both parents. Sometimes what parents do is entirely inappropriate for them and their children, and the result is usually an emotional garble of distress and unhappiness. Physical or emotional abuse, including sexual molestations, are extreme manifestations of parental incompetence. Not able to constructively resolve their own feelings of inadequacy, such parents subject their innocent children to perverted forms of power and authority.

Finally, it is common for parents to not enjoy their relationships with their children. Many of us believe that enjoying our children should be inherent. But I have seen many mothers and fathers who, for some reason or another, do not like their children and do not enjoy being around them. While they may feel quite guilty and frustrated, they are often unwilling to do what is necessary to learn how to love their own children. In order for us to develop a lasting love in marriage and to share the tasks of child rearing, each partner must be able to find rewards as a parent. I have seen difficulty arise when a wife, filled with the day's frustrations, would give her husband a negative report about the children as soon as he walked through the door from work. He would feel divided between his loyalty for his wife and his desire to have a good relationship with his children. Sometimes he would support his wife, ignoring the damage to his relationship with the children; other times he would work on his friendship with the children, ignoring his wife's comments. In this situation the wife could put off her complaints until later.

To this point, I have described some of the causes that make child care miserable. However, if couples can commit to improving their strategies, if they will apply to child care the tactics for building a lasting love, all aspects of family life will improve.

Child care should be a positive experience. If a couple are committed to making their love last, they will realize how important child care is to that goal. Not surprisingly, most skills used to develop a lasting love will also help in rearing children. Parents could project themselves forward to the day when their last child leaves home and ask such questions as "What am I glad I did with my children? Did I spend enough time with them? How did I treat them? Did I help them become what I wanted them to be?" Parents could then discuss how to achieve the answers they would want. Following is a list of areas they could discuss and suggestions for being effective in each area:

Deciding on Goals for Each Child

After thinking about what makes each child satisfied, parents could have a talking-and-listening session about objectives for their children. Couples need to be able to identify the characteristics they want most in their children, including such traits as emotional competence, affection, academic accomplishment, and loyalty. Parents may find that they cannot describe what they want because they do not have enough knowledge about children in general. They can find books to read, lectures to attend, or knowledgeable people to talk to. Deciding and participating together on the children's development will naturally lead to better understanding.

Agreeing on Rules and Consequences

A rule is any expected standard of behavior ranging from a family routine to a firm guideline about how children should perform at a given time, such as at meals or when cleaning a room. Since family rules will involve both parents, the mother and the father should discuss and agree on the setting up and enforcing of rules before attempting to implement them. Each partner should remember that the consequences of failure to agree are worse than adapting to the other person's point of view, unless the other person's view is actually destructive.

Sharing in the Supervision of Children

Both parents can participate in the supervision of children's performances, including their work at home, their school tasks, or any other thing a child does. When both parents notice a child's actions, discuss them with the child, and reinforce good behavior, the child benefits much more than when only one parent participates.

Sharing in Teaching Correct Behavior

Sometimes we let children alone until they do something wrong. Then we are forced to pay attention to what is undesirable. Teaching children how to behave correctly is much more effective (and fun). It is simply a matter of following these steps: (a) show them, (b) tell them, (c) encourage them to try it, (d) praise them.

Teaching Respect for Both Parents

To get their way, children will frequently attempt to divide their parents by saying, "But Dad (or Mom) said...," or they will tell one parent of their mistreatment at the hands of the other parent. If both parents are actively and positively sharing in child care, children will benefit when the parents make clear to them that (1) one parent will not allow the children to show disrespect for the other parent, (2) agreement between parents is more important than what the child wants to do, and (3) a child's criticism of the other parent may be understood, but it will not be acted upon in front of the children.

Finding Ways to Enjoy Children

Parents can benefit from identifying ways to increase their enjoyment of their children. They can dare to do some things with the family just because they want to. Sometimes parents believe in the necessity of continual sacrifice for the children rather than recognize that parents have the right to enjoy their children in ways that also contribute to their children's development.

For example, if we wish our children to do well in school, we can find a way to enjoy helping them do school work. This may sound like a contradication in terms, but helping a child with school projects can be very enjoyable. It can be a time filled with conversation, encouragement, and abundant praise, bringing parent and child closer.

I propose that child care is made more worthwhile through learning to enjoy our children. If we think through what will, at the same time, bring satisfaction to us and help our children grow, we can organize an effective child-care plan to follow.

Demonstrating Love for Each Other

Parents should also discuss and agree on the answer to this question: How shall we express our love in front of the children? Often the single best thing a parent can do for his or her children is to love the other parent. Indeed, observing affection between parents is very important for children. It sets an emotional climate beneficial to children, providing an example of the kind of behavior they will want to take into their marriages; in other words, it makes them happy now, and it will help them know how to be happy later.

Learning to share child care happily and confidently makes love between parents stronger; and their stronger love makes them even happier, better parents. Couples will find themselves creating a wonderful circle of marital satisfaction.

6

DISCOVERING NEW REWARDS

"I'm sorry I'm late," she whispered as they walked out to the car. She had taken one child to the doctor and another to a piano lesson. She had whipped up dinner for the children. Then, just as she was about to get herself ready, the fourth grader had announced a big school assignment. She had spent a few minutes helping him, and now she had no time left to bargain with. She would be late.

She didn't have to look to see if he was perturbed—his arm was unbending and his walk was stiff. "Uh-oh," she thought. He didn't say anything until they were in the car. Then he said to her loudly enough for their friends in the front seat to hear, "When are you ever going to be on time!" She explained her day's schedule but found, as always, that it didn't help. "You're just disorganized," he retorted. "Just once I wish you would be on time." She knew he was embarrassed because their friends had had to wait, and so she became silent. Why couldn't he be loyal to me, she thought, instead of criticizing me to make himself look good?

Their evening together was ruined. Later, at home, he even criticized her for being uninvolved and for spoiling the evening. They had had an opportunity to enjoy themselves together and had missed it. Had they been able to defer until later their expressions of disappointment in one another, they might have been able to enjoy their time together. As it was, his criticism and her silence made it unsatisfying. They failed to look for and find the rewards of being together.

We human beings are quite adaptable. We can even adapt to living with unhappiness. When we do adapt, we create a set of blinders that influence what we will see and believe in the future.

The reason for this is found in the role emotions play in human behavior. Our emotions stem from what we experience, but we remember experiences inseparably from the emotions that accompanied them: we remember what we felt. After we have had many experiences of different types, our brains classify them into categories. Emotions—sadness, anger, happiness—are the names of the categories in which our memories are stored. That is why one sad experience, for example, will trigger memories of other sad experiences.

Any couple will have some unrewarding experiences. If, however, there are many of these, they will collect in each partner's mind, affecting what each will think of his or her marriage. Then, any happy experiences that may happen will either be quickly forgotten or will seem strange or unrealistic. Unfortunately, unhappiness in marriage tends to create expectations for unhappiness, and the expectations tend to be met.

In order to shake loose from this cycle and to be free to find happiness in such a marriage, partners must look for, discover, and promote more rewarding marriage experiences, building up a category of loving memories. If more than half of the events the husband and wife share are rewarding, they will likely stay together. When fewer than half are rewarding, they begin to wonder if their efforts are worthwhile. Obviously, if their despair is too great, *nothing* will be rewarding. So trying to create more rewarding marital experiences is only appropriate for those who have enough commitment to want to try.

Looking for rewarding things is almost as important as actually finding them. If we concentrate on finding rewarding activities, we will be less likely to find the opposite. I remember talking with a young couple who had been married less than two years. They had been having a prolonged argument about some aspect of their marriage. Both of them said they didn't feel that their married life was rewarding. They felt that arguments meant they did not love each other. Their fear of failure showed in their faces, and I saw their discomfort and awkwardness. This argument they could not end had created for them a much greater problem—the possibility that their marriage would fail.

I asked them to recount how the argument had started. As they took turns recounting the series of arguments that had led to the present impasse, I pressed for more and more information about their feelings, the intensity of their reactions, and the frustration that encompassed them. After forcing them through one painful episode after another, I looked at both squarely and said, "You must love each other a great deal." Their surprise was obvious, and the husband voiced what I am sure both felt: "That is the last thing I thought you'd say."

I explained to him that, in a marriage relationship, love and commitment meant that each person could influence the other's feelings. I pointed out that their anger could not have been so intense nor their frustrations so great if they were not deeply in love. The emotional tension in the room eased immediately. Both became more relaxed, and I suggested to them that reducing the fears that their marriage was in serious trouble was the start to solving their conflict. As they left my office, I noticed that he reached for her hand and she gave it to him.

I had only been trying to help the two of them gain enough confidence to solve an ordinary marital problem. In the process of doing so, I made a discovery that has left me with a lasting impression. People often base their predictions about the future on their interpretation of the past. If a couple's past has been unhappy, they can become prisoners of unhappiness in the future merely through expecting their future to be unhappy. To break out of their shared misery, couples must learn how to discover or to create a more positive present for themselves in spite of the past.

LOOKING FOR REWARDS

Confronted by a husband who insisted that his marriage was unrewarding, I proposed that he ask several friends what they found rewarding in their marriages and make a list of what they said. He returned with over twenty-five items. He had frankly expected that few if any would find marriage rewarding, but saw that he was wrong. The next step was simple. He selected some items on the list and began to experiment. His story would have had a nice ending if I could report that to his surprise he had immediately found more rewards from his marriage. The truth is that his and his wife's growth have been gradual. They are still struggling to make their marriage more rewarding.

The next place to look for potential rewards is in family relationships. These can frequently come from changing our perspectives. One wife complained to her husband about small jammy handprints on the sliding glass door. Her husband looked up from his newspaper and said, "In thirty years we'll be willing to pay a hundred dollars for one small jammy handprint on our window. We had better enjoy them while we can." His wife immediately recognized the truth of his statement. Cleaning up a household mess had suddenly become a rewarding experience.

Social psychologists have identified several conditions that are inherently rewarding to human beings. These conditions satisfy us emotionally just as food satisfies us physically. They can be created or strengthened to help us find new rewards in marriage.

Interpersonal Attention

Interpersonal attention simply means that when we are attended to by someone else—when they compliment us, for example—we feel more expansive, more confident, and more expressive. Researchers have found that we keep talking longer when someone is paying attention to us. Attention also increases our enthusiasm for what we are saying and stimulates a more open expression of humor. Furthermore, attentiveness by a loved person stimulates arousal of the senses.

Interpersonal attention, then, acts upon our most positive characteristics. This attentiveness includes subtle signals like dilated pupils that increase the exposure of the eye to the view of others (women, using eye makeup to attract attention, have always known about this) as well as more obvious signals like touching or asking questions. This is why conversations when both talk and listen are so pleasant.

Warmth

One of the most interesting studies I have read reported that warmth is the one characteristic that both men and women prefer above all others in people they date. It is more attractive than physical beauty. Many of us have never learned to express warmth well, and it may take some effort to feel comfortable in doing it. But there is abundant evidence that increasing the amount of warmth we express increases the rewards we find in marriage.

Warmth is expressed in voice tones, in quiet physical contact, in praise, in the giving of small gifts or the performing of acts of service. Warmth is conveyed in greetings and good-byes. It is found in straightening mussed hair (or in mussing up neat hair). It is sometimes expressed merely by moving toward another person or by touching someone on the arm.

Warmth is partly related to what people expect—remembering important dates, for example. But surprises are even better. One wife knew of an important meeting her husband was to have one afternoon with some business associates and arranged to have a pink carnation delivered to his office that morning. The note with it read, "I have a pink passion for you." The meaning of the flower held some romantic promise as well as thoughtfulness. She knew how to send a message of warmth.

It is customary to think of men as being less warm than women, but I have found that they just express it differently. Men, for example, are more likely to give gifts or to do something for women. Women generally will express warmth through interpersonal attention. Everyone, I believe, can make his or her marriage more intimate by finding the rewards warmth can bring. One husband has a goal of expressing one new form of warmth every month. He says that meeting the goal has made him happier and has created a good climate at home.

Security and Peace

The security that comes from predictability and stability can be one of the most rewarding aspects of being married. One wife has said that she treasures her husband's ability to make her feel secure. The absence of suspicion and apprehension regarding her husband's activities gives her a great deal of satisfaction and peace.

We sometimes forget how important security and peace are to us; we may realize that we need it only when we don't have it. Most human beings do not function well under chronic periodic stress. If there is conflict, suspicion, or emotional pain in a marriage, the result can be insecurity and stress.

To increase the rewards we find in marriage, we may, for a time, have to agree that we will not incite each other to painful interchanges but instead will allow for times of quiet and peacefulness. Whenever we are filled with tension, whether from the marriage or from outside pressures, we will find it difficult to feel secure. In a sense, it is not actually money, or the in-laws, or the children, or any other commonly suggested cause that brings conflict into a marriage. It is the tension we feel and the resulting feeling of insecurity that are most often the causes of the conflict.

Companionship

There is something in us that makes us want to share our experiences with another person. Marriage affords us the ultimate opportunity for companionship, allowing us to share a multitude of experiences from shopping to vacations. Most people enjoy an experience more when another person sees and feels what they see and feel. Sharing what we experience stimulates our senses: it makes what we see, hear, taste, smell, and feel more intense than when we are alone.

I remember well a train ride down the Rhine Valley in Germany. As I traveled from Hamburg to Munich, I had a few extra hours and decided to take a small side trip through the valley. I was unprepared for how truly beautiful it was. The crystal clear river flowed slowly through the heavily wooded hills, which were interrupted occasionally by the silhouettes of ancient castles. Such peace and beauty were welcomed by most of the travelers on the train, but my reaction surprised me. I felt a great resentment and frustration that my wife could not witness what I was seeing. I felt as though I did not want to see another beautiful thing unless she could see it as well. I even felt a bit unfaithful having an experience that I knew she would have found exhilarating. Companionship took on a new and more significant meaning for me thereafter.

Response

We all find rewards in causing others to respond positively to us. In some marriages, the sterility of indifference creates a desperation that leads one partner, consciously or unconsciously, to repeatedly provoke the other. If positive provocation doesn't work, then a spouse may try negative provocation until he or she arouses some form of unhappy response.

I suppose a few people may actually prefer to cause unhappiness, but most of us would like to see someone else have joy as a result of what we do. Some people who have been constantly and heavily criticized may not feel able to bring happiness to the lives of other people. In contrast, those who lived with love and affection as children will likely assume that they can create warmth in the lives of others. I have a child who one day said something very funny during a family prayer. The resulting laughter encouraged him to try other humorous things. Most of them succeeded, so he was encouraged to believe that he could create laughter among people around him. Now, the ability to make people laugh has become a part of his personality.

We can find increased rewards in marriage when we attempt to converse, to compliment, to pay attention, and to love—all positive ways to invite a response from a spouse. There are many other techniques of "positive provocation" that we can find if we look for them. Trying them and receiving the consequent warm response will move us toward intimacy.

FINDING REWARDS IN SHARED RELIGION

I am not proposing that every couple be religious. It is true, however, that in most marriages, at least one partner will have had some form of religious training or experience, even if it is antireligious. My obective here is to suggest that, when shared in an amiable and positive way, religion can bring greater satisfaction and intimacy to marriage.

When husband and wives experience discord over religious practices, it is because they cannot find a comfortable way of sharing them. People of the same religion who participate at different levels of activity may also experience discomfort. Religious differences will not go away by themselves—some adjustment must be made to increase compatibility.

The easiest way for a couple to do this is to identify the religious activities available and calmly discuss the degree to which each partner is willing to participate. Rather than argue about the position taken by either person, a couple would be wise to focus on what each spouse wishes to do. To get the best results, a couple will need to make some accommodations. Spouses can learn that paying attention to each other at a religious activity can increase the rewards of marriage just the same as paying attention to each other at any other activity, such as a sports event. The important thing is to participate together and to do so in a way that rewards both.

I know of one wife who was actively involved in her religion. Her husband was not a member of her church. Although he allowed her to practice her religion freely, he did not actively participate either at home or at church. She wished that he would become more involved, and her encouragement on occasion amounted to a modest amount of pressure. She found, of course, that he resisted, and eventually he refused to participate even as much as he had done previously. One day she announced that her local congregation was organizing a marriage seminar consisting of two evening meetings for married couples. She did not mention that it featured a weekend retreat at a nearby conference center.

This was something that appealed to him, so he came with his wife to the meeting held at church. The conversation was informative and enjoyable. Following the lecture he was introduced to several of her friends, and, as she reported later, on the way home she found herself paying more attention to him and giving him more affection than usual. At the time neither one would have attributed her response to his participation with her. Both felt that it was due to the ideas they had learned during the meeting. At the second meeting he learned for the first time of the weekend retreat. The good experience with the two evening meetings led him to suggest attending the retreat. During the weekend he met and made friends with many members of his wife's church. Several weeks later a Christmas party was held for the adults of the congregation. He willingly came and participated in the evening's festivities.

What had once been a source of difficulty had now become an area of positive sharing. He still was not a member of her religion, but they had changed a difficult part of their marriage into one that offered reward and fulfillment. Without really knowing it, they had made the change by experiencing all the inherently rewarding conditions discussed earlier: attention, warmth, security, companionship, and response.

Since religious situations vary greatly, no one strategy is applicable to all situations. The table on the following page suggests five different strategies for finding rewards in shared religion.

There is considerable evidence that people with strong religious beliefs have more stable and satisfying marriage relationships than those without them. I believe the reason for this is that religious beliefs, when actively observed, create a sense of stability and depth and give continuity and consistency to two people's relationship. Stability is a key factor in enjoying marriage. Without it, upheaval and uncertainty can quickly lead to conflict. Evidence also suggests that marriages are more stable if couples are of similar faiths. While this is not a necessary condition for a happy marriage, it seems to contribute greatly to happiness.

Some couples may conclude from this that their marriages might improve if they sought out religions of their choice and jointly participated to the degree they found mutually satisfying. The resulting social and spiritual benefits may add a dimension to their lives that had not previously existed. As a counselor, I have suggested this course whenever it was proper for me to do so. In most cases, following this suggestion led couples to new rewards in their marriages that they had not imagined could exist.

Table 4
Religion and Rewarding Sharing Strategies

Situation	Strategy
Both spouses are equally active in one religion	A couple can place emphasis on getting the most from any participation. They can select appropriate activities that give them satisfaction and converse more often about religious topics.
Both spouses are equally active in different religions	All religions have some commonalities, and a couple can base their sharing on these. Partners can trade participation in important activities. If they avoid any participation in each other's religion, their sharing becomes negative. Friendly discussion and reassurances can be helpful.
Both spouses are unequally active in one religion	This is often the most difficult situation to share well. Pressure creates resistance, but pretending to participate (that is, participating without real belief or enjoyment) usually fails as well. The key is to decide on the minimum amount of shared participation and then work to make it rewarding.
Both spouses are unequally active in different religions	The more active partner can extend courtesies and invitations to the less active partner to participate, carefully avoiding pressure. The couple can also watch for important activities of interest in the church of the less active spouse. Both should make efforts to reinforce the importance of the marriage to each other.
Neither spouse is regularly involved in religious activity	If both spouses are indifferent to religion, their sharing will be based on other things. Each religious activity will require conversation and preparation because it will be unusual. In this situation, most arguments occur because one wishes to participate and the other does not. Spouses should honor and support each other's decision.

7

USING DIFFERENCES

People in troubled marriages often think that the cause of their unhappiness is the differences between them and their spouses. Whenever I hear this, I think how boring life would be if we were exactly like our marriage partners. In the first place, any man and woman will have differences just because one is male and the other female. In the second place, personality differences stemming from background and early family experiences will likely exist. People who live in satisfying marriages have as many differences between them as do people who are unhappy. The differences between us actually do not in themselves create any problems; the problems stem from the failure to see that differences are as much an opportunity for growth and happiness as they are a potential source of unhappiness.

When a couple allow differences to prevent mutually satisfying sharing in any of the important areas of marriage, they create a foundation for a lifetime of conflict. Rather than face differences that may arise, a couple may avoid each other in specific situations. For example, if the conflict is about money, a couple may decide that the husband will bring home the check, give it to his wife, and not talk about money again till the next paycheck. Or the wife may not feel comfortable about their sexual relationship but will continue to participate to avoid her husband's anger. One couple who came to my office had a problem with child care differences. The husband said, "We argued about how we should treat the kids, so we agreed that she would handle them and I would stay out of her way." Actually, this couple had agreed to perpetuate the differences and continue arguing. They might have temporarily decreased the frequency of their arguments, but they had not resolved their differences. Those differences would always exist as long as the couple avoided facing them. This couple's example is similar to many other couples.

IDENTIFYING AND RESOLVING DIFFERENCES

As I have said, couples face more than one type of difference in marriage. I want to propose here that successful resolution of a difference depends upon identifying the type of difference and responding to it appropriately. Generally, differences between husbands and wives can be divided into four categories. These are summarized in table 5 on the following page.

Nearly all differences between husbands and wives can be classified into at least one of these four categories, and a couple's strategy for resolving differences will be based on the type of difference itself. In the case of gender differences, for instance, couples can employ a strategy of accommodating each other, simply allowing each other the differences of being male and female.

In the case of deeply rooted personality traits, resolution of differences typically requires that both accept each other and calmly discuss the differences openly. Behavior closely tied to a long-standing system of values and beliefs is extremely resistant to change, so, rather than resist and argue, a couple will do better to look for ways to benefit from the differing beliefs and values. In this process, they will find that *any* value system has positive characteristics.

Differences in specific situations represent the most frequent type of marital difference. The best strategy for resolving such differences is to develop an ongoing system of reconciliation that requires behavior change in both spouses. A husband who is shy, for example, may find less interest in social get-togethers than his wife. The couple can adjust quite happily if both compromise somewhat, the husband making more effort to go out and enjoy group dates, the wife scheduling fewer such

Table 5
Understanding Differences

Type of Difference	How They Are Expressed	Suggestions for Responses
Gender differences	Gender differences are traits that distinguish most males in a group from most females. They may be physical or cultural. For example, wives in North American society tend to want more discussion with their husbands about feelings than husbands tend to want.	One person should yield to the spouse's wishes at appropriate times.
Deeply rooted values	Deeply rooted values or beliefs are expressed in a person's general behavior. They are most clearly seen in the priorities people establish. Examples include a person's religious practices and a person's beliefs about how formally or informally one should present himself socially.	Both spouses should accommodate and freely accept but should also discuss each other's values.
Differences in specific situations	Personality differences are expressed in certain situations. Examples include one spouse talking more openly with friends while being silent around strangers, or a spouse being fastidious at work but less so at home.	Compromise and conciliation are possible. Both must expect to make some changes.
Personal mannerisms	These are small personality quirks expressed as by-products of other actions. They may include facial expressions or a manner of speech that changes occasionally.	A couple can change through bargaining.

events. One of the great ironies of marriage is that oftentimes the behavior we deem inappropriate in our partner is either stimulated or reinforced by how we act. Therefore, to modify a partner's behavior, a person must also make a change in himself. A couple must remember that through changes personal growth takes place, and they become better people.

Personal mannerisms are usually more a form of annoyance than a source of real difference between spouses. Yet their significance can be great if the atmosphere of a marriage is charged with hostility, disappointment, or other negative emotions. In many cases a couple can resolve an annoyance if the observer will discreetly point out the mannerism to the spouse and ask for a change. Care should be taken not to hurt the spouse's feelings. Sometimes coexistence—simply allowing the mannerism to exist and not criticizing it—is best, especially when a mannerism is so habitual as to be difficult to change. Quite frequently once-annoying mannerisms become endearing when attention is focused on loving the person and not on insignificant behavior.

THE POSITIVE USE OF DIFFERENCES

A couple can begin to use their differences in positive ways if they can agree to the following steps: First, they must be willing to give up belittling or criticizing each other, defending themselves, and explaining in response to comments. Most can simply stop—they do not need a miracle or a terrible argument to motivate them. Criticizing people for annoying traits or belittling them for mistakes produces justification, defense, and elaborate explanation. This cycle will perpetuate the status quo and will not result in any constructive change. The first requirement, therefore, is to stop the cycle. The cycle itself accomplishes nothing: criticism does not promote behavioral change, and defensiveness does not stop criticism. If the initiator—the criticizer—won't stop, the receiver of criticism can still help by refusing to be defensive, though this takes great strength.

Second, a couple must be honest with each other. A husband and wife especially need to recognize the true nature of the difference between them. To accomplish this, a couple must be willing to examine each other's viewpoints and to create a "nonthreatening" atmosphere. One woman was married to a man who enjoyed making fun of her in front of their friends. Thinking he would soon stop, she patiently let him make her the butt of his jokes, but he kept on. She finally decided to talk it over with him. She prepared him by saying that she wanted to talk about something unpleasant and wished him to "listen kindly." Then she explained what she had observed and told him she was hurt whenever he did it. She asked if he could stop doing it. He attempted to pass off her statement by joking about it, but when she persisted, he knew she meant what she said. He agreed to change and found it was not difficult.

Third, a couple must understand that any discussion to resolve a difference has one central objective: to find a way of satisfying both spouses. Any resolution of differences is judged by whether it will produce happiness or fulfillment for both people. Successful couples find many ways to express this idea to each other. Satisfying both partners is central to the process of using differences to improve the marriage.

MANAGEMENT OF MONEY AND RESOURCES

The most frequently discussed difference of opinion in marriage has to do with the management of money and resources. For success in money management a couple must first demonstrate the maturity to reduce the criticism and defensiveness they have manifested in previous arguments about money, and then take time to honestly understand the differences between them. A couple should understand that there are several ways couples could successfully manage their finances. They need only find one that helps both feel satisfied and regulates the flow of money adequately.

One difference, of course, centers around the issue of who controls or makes decisions about the use of available money. Traditionally, a husband may feel that managing the funds is a husband's prerogative, or his wife may claim the right because she sees herself as the better manager. Another frequent difference is related to each person's viewpoint of time. Some people would rather spend their money now to acquire things for the present, while others would prefer to save for some future purchase. Another common money difference relates to different personal values. One person may value material possessions, preferring to buy nice cars, homes, or clothes, while the other may be more interested in personal growth, using money for music lessons, pottery classes, family vacations, or college educations. Another frequent argument concerning money revolves around maintaining a public image or achieving private satisfaction. Some people wish to maintain a social position that requires a home and facilities equal to or better than the local standard. This becomes a source of conflict when someone with this orientation is married to someone who doesn't care about what other people think and who wants to put the money into less conspicuous areas.

Differences may also be evident in the ways people try to manage their money. A difference between spouses may exist, for example, in what they believe to be "good" and "bad" management. One reared in a family that operated on a budget and kept track of all expenditures may be fearful of a more flexible management system in which a budget or a record is not kept. The person who likes the more rigid system of money management is frightened that the flexible method will result in a squandering of resources. The one who favors the looser style becomes frustrated that the conservative person is so tight. The situation could have serious repercussions. The one who has a more conservative management style may become more cautious and tend to put off buying luxuries and even necessities. The one who is more flexible may make decisions more freely and purchase things impulsively.

Once money differences (there is almost always more than one) are understood, a couple can determine whether they stem from gender preferences, deeply rooted values and beliefs, or personality traits expressed in specific situations. Then an appropriate strategy for resolving the differences can be devised.

RESOLVING MONEY DIFFERENCES

As a couple devises a strategy, they must realize that the only acceptable solution is one that will satisfy both. In fact, a couple should say this and agree to it openly, more than once, and with great sincerity. They should also decide to work on only one issue at a time.

> *Step 1.* A husband and wife should say what they want to do with the money and what they expect from each other. This conversation is to clarify and promote understanding. Example: Wife—"I want us to save, to keep detailed books, and to pay cash for most of what we buy." Husband, after showing he has listened—"I can't stand all that detail. I want to have the feeling of being able to buy what I want to when I want to."
>
> *Step 2.* A couple should then answer the question, "What will happen if I give you exactly what you want?" Example: Wife—"If we do what you want, I think we'll have more freedom, but I will be more afraid." Husband—"Yes, but if we follow your system, you will feel secure, but I'll feel trapped."
>
> *Step 3.* A couple could then work out an adjustment, trying to find a mutually satisfactory solution. Example: Wife—"Let's see if we can set up two categories of spending. We'll be detailed for some things and flexible for others." Husband—"Then both of us will be detailed, and both will have more freedom."
>
> *Step 4.* A couple should then try out what they have agreed to do, setting a time for future evaluation. For instance, they may decide to try the new system for thirty days. For other kinds of differences, they may have to set up a day-to-day evaluation and reinforcement procedure. They may, for example, reward themselves on successful days and penalize themselves on unsuccessful days. If previous conflicts about money have been vigorous or volatile, the day-to-day approach is usually helpful. Once a couple realizes a change of behavior, they may then go on to another specific issue and resolve it.

The successful resolution of any difference is based on the premise that differences are as useful and interesting as they are problematic. Every couple will find that calmly resolving differences will bring added satisfaction to their relationship.

8

REDUCING ANGER

Many people believe that expressing anger is a good way to get rid of it. I am not sure that that is a good idea in any situation, and I am convinced that it is almost always inappropriate in marriage. Expressing anger in violent, explosive ways feeds the anger, increasing the chances that we will "blow up" again. The ways we act, speak, or feel will frequently entrench themselves in the marriage relationship because of ours and our spouses' responses and reinforcement. This happens whether the behavior is good or bad.

It is not realistic to assume that we will never get angry. It is usually better to expect anger and plan to deal with it in a way that does not add to our problems. Most anger in marriage comes from the idea that our spouse is not loyal, loving, or as attentive as we deserve and is *choosing* to be that way. It is the thought of conscious neglect that incites us. When we are given a good reason for someone's infuriating behavior, such as a handicap or ignorance, our anger diminishes. If we are wise, therefore, we will try hard to understand and to adapt to the *sources* of our marital anger.

When couples are not able to do this for one reason or another, they find that, whenever the anger-provoking situation recurs, the anger returns. Some couples believe that, if they do not talk about the explosive issues, the issues will go away, but no solutions are found this way. The people who feel that anything is better than having an argument fail to realize that avoiding the situation only forces anger underground. The problems we do not solve come up again and again; that is the nature of marriage. Failing to find resolutions produces hidden resentment that results in emotional distance. This hidden resentment can be lifelong. Such situations are avoidable because people who correctly understand the source of problems and correctly adapt to them can usually find solutions.

ANGER AND THE MARRIAGE RELATIONSHIP

At this point we should note that marriage itself is a condition that can increase the likelihood of conflict. One reason for this is that marriage will naturally involve us in what is most important to us and will lower our threshold of control through the stresses of such responsibilities as child rearing, sexual relationships, and money management. (This is why many people experience more peace and less anger during trial separations. Then when they attempt life together again, they find that their separation has produced no lasting positive results.) Because this intensity is inherent in virtually all marriages, we could conclude that personal limitations might be exacerbated by marriage unless people mature emotionally and adjust properly to them.

I want to discuss here three sources of anger in marriage: (1) personal problems of one spouse or both, (2) self-defeating relationship styles, and (3) external pressures.

Personal Problems

Personal problems that affect the marriage relationship may range from an actual physical disability to a tendency to suffer from certain moods. Many personal problems can prevent full participation in the marriage relationship. As an example, one woman I know had an extremely authoritarian and abusive father. She had been glad to leave home and had become a competent and successful young adult. However, as she began to date her prospective husband and as her feelings for him deepened, she began to experience considerable amounts of anxiety. This anxiety was characterized by irrational criticisms of her fiance's behavior.

She also felt so controlled by the relationship that she often wanted to escape and would withdraw, sulk, or pout. The couple resolved these problems well enough to gain confidence that they would enjoy being married. But when their sexual relationship began in marriage, she found that she could not respond warmly to his affection. The closer he came to establishing intimacy, the more frightened she became. Because he could not see how he was a direct part of the problem, he became angry at his wife's inability to act in an expected or normal way. His resentment, of course, worsened the problem, and she grew more afraid of her husband's insensitivity and frustration.

Another common personal problem that can invite anger into marriage is depression. When a person experiences prolonged periods of depression, he or she is unable to be fully involved or to function well in marriage. Even though a spouse may respond with empathy and sensitivity (which, incidentally, can sometimes worsen the situation), resentment begins to build and eventually may explode into anger.

Other personal problems that affect a marriage may include excessive alcohol consumption, drug abuse, physical injury, or the inability to organize one's schedule to allow time for sustaining the marriage relationship. One example of the last problem comes from the life of a physician who had created a successful medical practice. The doctor felt a considerable obligation to his patients. He had reason to feel obligated; his work was important. He believed it required long hours at three different hospitals and kept him busy from early morning to late at night. Having endured this for years, his wife finally got angry and threatened divorce.

His marriage was nearly saved when he became seriously ill with a viral infection. His confinement and recuperation gave the two of them time to talk about their marriage and to be involved with each other. Unfortunately, when he recovered, he quickly returned to his previous schedule. She quite correctly interpreted this as an indication that he felt more strongly about his patients and medical practice than he did about his marriage. She is now living with their children in their new, huge, and beautiful home. He is living alone in a small apartment near one of the hospitals.

If the personal limitations of marriage partners are relatively insignificant, are manifested rarely or temporarily, or are easily remedied, most couples can easily maintain a positive marital balance. If the limitations amount to chronic problems, however, anger will also compound the problems, and solutions will be more difficult to find.

If an offended spouse can see no remedies for a partner's problem, he or she will often decide to dissolve the marriage. But high praise should go to those who can choose a better option—to live in a less than satisfying marriage. These generous people are required to adjust their expectations and emotional needs and to do it without complaint. Such sacrifice can lead to a deeper understanding of faithfulness and love. Unfortunately, that understanding is not obtained easily and is not something all can attain. The choice to stay or to leave a marriage plagued by a chronic personal problem is among the most difficult choices anyone could make.

Relationship Styles

When the famous anthropologist Margaret Mead first began her observations of primitive tribes in New Guinea, her husband Gregory Bateson, also an anthropologist, traveled with her. We know less about him than about his wife because his work was in a more specialized field than hers, but he made significant contributions to understanding human relationships. He learned that all two-person relationships form styles of shared behavior that become habitual. He acquired his knowledge about relationship styles by watching how the members of the three prominent tribes treated each other.

He wrote that when the members of tribe A went to the village of tribe B, tribe A yelled and shook their spears and shields, and tribe B became increasingly submissive. Instead of placating the anger of tribe A, tribe B's submissiveness led to more agitation. In response to the increased agitation, the members of tribe B became even more submissive. This spiral of dominance and submission continued until the members of tribe

A became so angry that one of them threw a spear, killing a member of tribe B.

Dr. Bateson did not fully understand what he was observing until, at a later time, he watched the members of tribe A visit the village of tribe C. When tribe A shook their spears, yelled, and rattled their shields, tribe C responded with identical behavior. This response stimulated tribe A to become even louder and more vicious, which drew a like response from tribe C. Their mutual anger escalated until a member of one of the tribes threw a spear and started a small skirmish, resulting in the death and injury of members of both tribes.

Dr. Bateson watched these events take place between the tribes on many different occasions. He concluded that people form relationship styles that tend to be habitual. Once learned, these styles continue to be acted out again and again. He identified a relationship style in which two participants exchange *opposite* behavior. That is, if one were dominant, the other would be submissive. If one were quiet, the other would be talkative. If one were clean, the other would be messy. If one were shy, the other would be gregarious.

When behavior is paired together often enough, as it tends to be in marriage, one person's behavior becomes a stimulus for the other's behavior. This means that the more dominating a husband might become, the more submissive the wife would be in response. Or the more the wife wanted to talk, the more quiet he would become. Dr. Bateson called this relationship style *complementary* because the two parties exchanged (or traded) opposite actions.

A couple with a complementary relationship style will face a sense of rigidity and control that stifles their freedom. Furthermore, such a style often leads to anger. For example, if one spouse is a dominating force, the other spouse develops ways to resist or to not respond. When the dominant partner demands a response, the other spouse will often resist by being late for appointments or by being passive. The dominant person, for instance, may ask the other to perform a simple task, but the submissive person appears to forget, resulting in the dominant person's anger.

Couples with strong complementary behavior have a unique pattern of arguing: one gives reasons, rationale, lessons, and sermonettes, while the other remains subdued. If the subdued spouse does not respond at all, the more outgoing person becomes even angrier and more frustrated, condemning the other for lack of response. The active spouse invariably forgets that the passive person is passive because the dominant person is dominant.

Couples should remember that both spouses act to create a complementary relationship. In a dominant/submissive relationship, one spouse cannot be dominant unless the other is submissive, nor can one spouse be submissive unless the other is dominant.

Gregory Bateson identified the second relationship style as one featuring identical or similar behavior. In the second style couples or groups develop *symmetrical* relationships. A couple with this style exchange identical actions—blaming, attempting to control, talking, not talking, approaching, withdrawing—one person in response to the other. For such a couple, any action may trigger a symmetrical response, even a positive action. One couple of my acquaintance reported that early in their marriage they had difficulty saying "I love you" to each other. The reason for this was that, if one spouse said, "I love you," the other spouse felt required to reciprocate. It became frustrating for one to say, "I love you," while the other felt forced to respond with "I love you, too." They both sensed a reduction in freedom. They attempted to solve this problem by not expressing their love for each other. Finally one suggested that for a brief period they agree to not respond in kind to declarations of love. When the husband told his wife he loved her, she remained silent or expressed her reaction by a touch or gesture. Gradually they changed their symmetrical relationship style into something more satisfying.

The emotions in a symmetrical relationship tend to be unstable, even volatile. There is intense competitiveness, and both spouses scrutinize each other's behavior, often resorting to mutual criticism and blame. Over a period of time, each accumulates an arsenal of verbal weapons. Like those in a complementary relationship, couples within a symmetrical one have a unique style of conflict: when an argument occurs, it starts with something relatively minor and escalates gradually, each spouse saying increasingly hurtful things until both spouses reach their limits in anger and frustration.

I watched an argument like this in my office. As I watched with great surprise, the wife accused her husband of being unable to provide properly for herself and the children. He responded that he did not feel motivated to provide for a wife who was frigid. She countered by suggesting that she could never be responsive to someone who was as unclean as her husband. He acknowledged his lack of cleanliness but suggested it was caused by her inability to organize the house, especially his clothes. This dialogue continued with escalating anger until she announced that she was no longer willing to tolerate his insults and would leave him. He had a response equal to his wife's threat: he simply said, "Good." She then countered by saying, "Oh, no, you don't. You want me to be the one to leave and be the guilty person." She announced that she would not be the one to leave the marriage, and they concluded their argument with angry silence.

Obviously, it does not matter what is talked about in either a complementary or a symmetrical argument. The issue is not the topic of conversation but the style of interaction that baits and catches both. Couples with these relationship styles have rehearsed their exchanges so frequently that their arguments have fallen into habitual patterns. Typically, both partners loyally carry out their roles even though they may both be unsatisfied by them.

Modest amounts of complementary and symmetrical interaction appear in most marriages. But when there is too much of either, the relationship is unhealthy and unhappy. Seeing someone responding exactly as you act or exactly opposite from the way you act does not create happiness. In both complementary and symmetrical relationships, couples are usually aware that they are caught in repetition, but they feel they can do little to break out of it. The anger comes from the habitual nature of the exchanges.

Stress from External Events

Yet another source of anger comes from events outside the marriage that increase stress or pressure, which in turn intensifies emotions. For example, pressures from work may be brought home in the form of frustration and simmering anger. This reduces the person's patience, and any arguments that occur are primarily attempts to release the preexisting stress. Another example is when one partner faces many tasks to be performed in a short period of time. Trying to get everything accomplished results in stress, increasing the likelihood of frustration and anger.

Relationships with friends and relatives, if unhappy, could also be considered sources of external pressure. One couple earned their livelihood by participating in a family business. The husband worked daily with other members of his immediate family, who also expected him to participate in family reunions and other family activities monthly. So demanding was this schedule that the wife correctly felt that he was unduly influenced by *his* family and not committed or involved enough in *their* family. The external pressure that he felt from his family and that she felt from his busy schedule caused their anger.

Sometimes external pressures are caused by events beyond our control. These may include loss of a job or a move in order to change a job. Other examples include neighborhood problems, children's problems at school, events that cause social embarrassment, or demands made because of church membership.

The point to remember is that external pressures overload emotions and increase the likelihood of anger. At first we may fail to recognize the source of pressure and mistakenly assume that someone else, such as a spouse or child, is the problem. In that case we misplace our anger, directing it to someone else who is innocent. As we mature, we can more easily recognize external pressure and can attempt to defuse our responses to it. If we are successful, we keep ourselves healthy and our homes more peaceful. If we fail, however, the sense of our inadequacy makes us even more vulnerable to the effects of stress.

WHAT WE CAN DO

My purpose in describing problems is to help a couple recognize them more easily. When we identify a marital problem early and accurately, we go a long way toward avoiding married lives plagued by confusion and frustration. More importantly, we can plan our responses to the problems. Most people with a history of problems also have a history of attempted solutions that failed. Table 6 will help identify types of marital problems and their possible solutions:

Table 6
Marital Problems and Solutions

Problem	Identifying Characteristics	Possible Solutions
Personal Problems	A person suffers from behavior or from moods that prevent him from participating fully in ordinary marital activities. A mood or behavior can be periodic, such as depression, or chronic, such as behavior arising from injury.	The spouse without the problem must avoid too much involvement with or too strong a reaction to the spouse with the problem. The couple must achieve a good balance between what they do separately and what they do together.
Relationship styles: 1. Complementary style	Spouses act in opposite ways. They feel a strong loss of freedom and spontaneity. Their relationship style escalates toward increased rigidity and bitterness. In arguments one person is active and the other is passive.	A couple can increase the variety of what they do together and what they talk about. They can rehearse for specific situations responses that break their pattern of argument.

Problem	Identifying Characteristics	Possible Solutions
2. Symmetrical style	The spouses' behavior patterns are identical. The couple's relationship escalates toward increased emotional instability. In arguments couples trade criticisms. Arguments are poorly resolved and can be stopped only by withdrawal.	A spouse can try behaving in new ways. A couple can rehearse noncombative responses and use them at critical times during arguments. A couple can give each other permission in advance to act as they are already acting (i.e., "When I talk loud, it's all right if you talk loud too").
External pressure	The source of the pressure is usually recognizable, but before it is correctly identified, it frequently results in misplaced and immaturely expressed anger. Sometimes the anger is accompanied by withdrawal and self-pity. Spouses may feel that they no longer have control over their lives.	A couple can (1) identify the source of the pressure, (2) attempt to alter it or its effects, (3) work to increase positive and pleasurable activities together, and (4) learn ways to insulate the marriage and family from the stress of external events.

I mentioned earlier that problems have a better chance to be solved by correctly matching a solution to the problem. The information provided in Table 6 shows that each problem must be met by a different solution.

Solving Personal Problems

Quite frequently, when a person is experiencing personal problems, the spouse becomes the caretaker or the "problem solver." Often, the problem solver's attempts to help are met by increased frustration, compounding the problem. It is usually better for the spouse without the problem to remain separate by (1) acknowledging there is a problem, (2) expressing concern, (3) offering availability if needed, and (4) not getting involved.

If attempts to help are not actually helpful, then an ugly

pattern can evolve. The "disabled" person may actually begin using the problem to get attention, and the problem will continue as long as one spouse receives numerous responses from the other.

The suggested solution for personal problems is for the couple to maintain a healthy balance between separateness and togetherness. Suppose, for example, that a wife has episodes of depression. Her husband has attempted to help her out of the depression by doing things around the house and responding warmly and affectionately to her desires. Some of his actions may be appropriate, but they can lead to a habitual situation. It would be better for the husband to say that he notices his wife's situation and is therefore not insensitive and that he has a desire to help her and will do so whenever she requests help. This places responsibility for the solution of the problem on the person who has the problem. When this person must ask for help or must ask for some sort of support, the likelihood of anger between the two is reduced. The task for the spouse without the problem is to remain outside the problem area until the "emotionally disabled" person has taken some responsibility.

Another possible solution for a personal problem is to enlarge the discussion and explanation of it. Quite frequently one person carries an emotional problem from the past into the marriage and has tried to solve it privately. The spouse may be keeping the problem from open scrutiny and may continue to harbor false beliefs or unresolved attitudes. Part of the solution of a personal problem comes from a person explaining and talking about the problem, assuming responsibility for it, and using the partner only as a source of clarification and understanding. This allows the spouse without the problem to remain separate, help more effectively, and avoid anger.

Improving Relationship Styles

The proposed solution for anger stemming from a relationship style is fairly self-evident. If we increase the number of different ways we act toward each other, we are less likely to be caught in either a complementary or a symmetrical pattern. A couple could participate in new and different, even adventurous, activities and try new ways of acting in old situations. If a couple recognize that they both create the problem, they can cooperate in increasing the number of ways they act toward each other. Quite frequently some very specific situations, such as mealtimes or conversations about the children, are linked to complementary or symmetrical exchanges. It may be that the only time anger occurs in the relationship is at these specific times. Knowing this, a couple can decide exactly what they want to do in that specific situation, rehearse it, and, when the situation arises, carry out their new "noncomplementary" or "nonsymmetrical" behavior. Rehearsing for specific situations is an effective way to reduce the negative effects of relationship styles.

Reducing Stress from External Events

The start to solving problems stemming from external pressure is to identify the sources of stress. A couple can then work on alleviating the stress, being careful not to focus so much on the source of stress that they forget to have positive and satisfying experiences together. If they allow themselves to worry more about external things than about positive marital interaction, they will develop new problems and fail to create mutual support. When a couple face financial strain, for example, they can organize mutual activities that give both of them comfort and satisfaction. Although this does not directly solve the problem, it effectively reduces feelings of anger.

A couple can also increase the frequency of discussion about the stressful circumstances. Quite often a spouse will react to external pressure by keeping his or her family from it, secretly carrying all or part of the burden alone. A couple that frequently discuss the problem can develop the feeling that they are mutually working toward a solution. The reassurance both spouses feel because they are not alone will improve their ability to deal with the problem, and the closeness of working together will create a stronger bond.

Anger arising from problems is almost always an enemy of marital happiness. A couple can reduce the feelings and expression of anger through early and accurate recognition of problems, the maintenance of positive marital activities, and the knowledge that anger from problems is destructive. Many couples forget to solve their problems because each spouse is angry at the other for getting angry. Most of us do not function well when we hear or see someone else's anger. Expressions of anger tend to increase apprehension, which reduces effectiveness. When we diminish our anger by working to solve our problems, we increase the likelihood that we will be more steadfast in our marriage, achieving an actual change of behavior that can improve the quality of our lives.

9
ACCEPTING WITH HOPE

A marriage flows along on a stream of time. It has a past, present, and future. Few of us truly realize that the way we view time affects the quality of the relationship. For instance, if a couple habitually recall and discuss unhappy memories, the sadness of the past will influence what they feel in the present. Likewise, if a person over-idealizes how things should or will be, his appreciation of what is actually happening in the present will be hindered.

Of all the attitudes we can have about marriage, two are especially important as touchstones of happiness: *hope*, belief that gradual improvements can be made as time passes; and *acceptance*, recognition and adaptation without blame or criticism. Linked together, these two attitudes can turn time into a powerful ally for marriage. Accepting with hope means bringing everything good from the past and the future to bear on the present.

I am not sure why we form illusions that prevent us from knowing exactly what is going on. I do know that people who are angry at their spouses, troubled about some aspect of their marriage, or just generally depressed fail to perceive reality. On occasion, I have asked someone in one of those categories to close his eyes and tell me how many pictures are on the walls of my office and how many plants are in the room. Even those who have been in the room several times fail to answer correctly. "What else are you missing?" I ask. When such a person is pressed to make more careful observation, he always finds that a great deal in his life has gone unnoticed, so focused was he on pain and trouble. Sometimes, after realizing this much, a person can take the next step to learn what he fails to understand.

ACCEPTANCE

Some couples live together as virtual strangers because they are unskilled in learning about each other. One or both spouses may be unable to talk personally or to be sensitive to each other's thoughts or feelings. Another person may focus so restrictedly on certain actions, such as expressions of nonloving behavior, that he or she will ignore all other actions. A common example of this is a man who has learned to focus so much on getting things done that he becomes concerned only about external productivity and cannot or will not recognize another person's—or even his own—feelings or motives. Such a man will discuss the need to be organized, while his wife feels misunderstood and unaccepted. Still other people are unwilling to spend the time necessary to learn about and understand a spouse and to maintain intimacy in the marriage.

Acceptance implies that we are willing to learn about another person, that we will *notice*. It also implies that we are willing to suspend judgment on our spouses' personalities and actions. As children, we probably learned to judge things by standards of good and bad, right and wrong. As adults, we expanded our judgment categories to include logical and illogical, rational and emotional. In marriage we may keep trying to fit our partners into one of these categories. All too frequently spouses will judge their partners to be "bad" or "illogical" at a time when their partners are just being themselves. Acceptance means understanding other people's reasons for behaving, and allowing them to act without judging them by our standards.

To illustrate how ludicrous judgments can be, consider the wife who says, "Gee, it's cold in here," while her husband seriously replies, "Oh, you're wrong. I'm so warm I feel like opening the window." Like many of us, he is assuming that if he feels something, he is right. If he is warm, someone who claims to be cold must be wrong. But he is trying to do the impossible: judge another's personal experience by his own. All of us are unique: we possess a set of lifetime experiences peculiar to ourselves, our own values, and our own personalities. When we choose to voice them or share them in other ways, acceptance requires that we suspend all judgment and attempt to understand. This only requires a little pause and an effort to seek for more information.

Acceptance also requires showing consistent warmth. I first became fully aware of this in a classroom discussion as a college student. While I was expressing an opinion, a fellow student nodded, smiled, and appeared interested in what I was saying. I felt his encouragement and support, but when I finished, he asked a question to clarify some point and then said, "I disagree with you." My first reaction was surprise, followed by a feeling of betrayal. As I thought about it later, however, I realized that he had been warmly attentive despite his disagreement. This characteristic was something I wanted to acquire, because I knew that when I did not approve of or did not agree with someone, I was less attentive to and less concerned about him.

Many married people display a warm involvement only when all is easy and is going well. They do not realize that such judgmental involvement leads their partners to say only what might be acceptable, so as to avoid rejection. Those who fear the withdrawal of warmth learn to close themselves and to not give all of themselves to a marriage. Many men who are stingy or inconsistent with warmth do not understand why their wives become less spontaneous and interested in them.

To succeed at warmth, we can learn to treat it as something that is always present because we are always willing to show it. By expressing care for the other person before discussing the issue, warmth, as part of acceptance, can be sustained even when conflict arises. The following examples show how this idea can be applied:

> A wife has had an accident that crumpled the rear fender and bumper of her car. Her husband sees the car in the garage before he sees his wife. He asks first about her welfare and then about the accident, listening to her explanation and expressing gratitude for her safety. (No

> amount of anger will reduce the cost of the repairs, even if the accident was her fault.)
>
> An overly stressed husband reacts improperly and angrily to his children. His wife hustles them out of his path, avoiding entering into the fray. Then she begins to comfort him by asking if he wants to talk, wants to rest, or wants to be alone. She tells of her care for him. (If she gets angry at him, he will only get angrier.)
>
> A miscommunication results in a husband waiting for his wife for two hours at the wrong place. He expresses his frustration at the situation without accusing his wife of stupidity. He waits until he is calmer and then opens a discussion about how to prevent such a miscommunication from happening again. (Anger and accusation will only arouse defensiveness and hurt feelings.)

Acceptance has many benefits for marriage. It reduces the number of arguments because neither spouse feels judged or accused. Often this is the reason some couples can honestly say they do not argue with each other. Acceptance increases a couple's desire to be together. It reduces pressure and increases freedom since each spouse can determine on his own what he wants to be and wants to do. Frequently the absence of pressure increases a couple's desire for each other's companionship. Acceptance also increases the amount of security a spouse feels. If we want to feel more secure, we can do so not by trying to get others to accept us, but by beginning to accept others more.

ACCEPTANCE AND HOPE

I first learned about the importance of hope in marriage from a woman in her middle twenties. She was pretty and articulate but very unhappy. She had been happily and excitedly in love when she married three years earlier, but now she claimed to have no love for her husband. She could recall many happy times in her marriage before the day she told her mother about her wonderful sex life. Her mother cautioned her that being too aggressive sexually might be unbecoming. Futhermore, occasional comments from close relatives about her husband's "crude" eating habits or "funny" way of pronouncing some words finally began to affect her. This susceptible young woman started to notice these traits for the first time. She let them annoy her and began to withdraw her feelings from her husband, not only because of her negative thoughts, but also because she was thinking about him in an impersonal, almost clinical way. Eventually she concluded that she did not love him anymore and that she had no hope to ever love him again.

We might think her very immature to be so easily influenced. Hopefulness, however, is delicate, and for some of us it can be easily lost. If we concentrate on what is lacking in others, we will not keep trying to become better, and we will be unlikely to give them the encouragement they need to improve. Hope is found in the praise or compliments we give—"You do that very well"—to people who are not always as good at something as they could be. We praise because we believe, and hope that what is less than perfect will get better.

Statements of love for each other and refusal to criticize also convey hope. If we acknowledge the love we feel today, we create hope that love will continue in the future. When we experience enough hopeful moments in the present, we can share a belief that our marriage will succeed, and this belief will give us the strength to travel through rough spots ahead.

HOPE AND HAPPINESS

Many people would not be willing to stake their happiness on something as intangible as hope. More often people consider basing their happiness on something more tangible, such as money, a nice home, or a social life. While such things may be important, some people are quite happy without any of these tangible supports. Indeed, each person's source of happiness is to some degree unique: what each of us is willing to rely on or to believe in may be different. Nevertheless, it is hopefulness—simple and sometimes subtle hope—that triggers the sense of happiness in all of us.

If couples in conflict could live one day together without

conflict—without discussing sad memories, without blaming each other, without wishing for the perfect person whom neither will ever become—they would feel at the day's end a small ripple of hope that tomorrow could be even better. Just a little bit of hope makes a spouse feel safer from unkindness and secure enough to risk small gestures of affection. With that, the sending and receiving of messages of love become possible. As we are *warmed* by love, the hurt begins to fade. "It just might work," we think. "We might make it this time," an inner voice tells us. Even with setbacks, hope gives us the strength to try again. Our happiness increases because we begin to have confidence that whatever is good will remain.

Many married couples have times of despair, but they try again and through their efforts find more happiness. Unfortunately many people do not realize that their hope is what improved their feelings. If we could recognize the encouragement we get from hope, we would be more eager to find it and reduce the unhappiness we feel at times. How much effort do we need to make to say a few words of encouragement, to show some warmth, or to use a few gestures of caring? How difficult is it to ignore some hurtful memory in favor of a more pleasant memory? How much strain do we feel when we take time to listen, understand, and accept? We need only the will and consistency to do these things. On the other hand, recovery from the spiteful words we say, from rejection and critical judgments, or from withdrawal is much more difficult.

We can easily generate hope for ourselves that living together will be increasingly enjoyable. We need only recognize that happiness results from the hope expressed when we share pleasant things and when we show love at times we do not have to or at times our partner cannot.

Many marriages need not fail. We do need to not do the hurtful things humans are capable of doing when they do not care. We do not have to consign ourselves to the loneliness of divorce if we will believe in and rely on the hope that comes from communicating that we love each other, what we appreciate in each other, and when we feel attracted to each other.

INDEX